"Todd Duncan is a great motivator with consistently excellent content. *High Trust Selling* is the embodiment of what Todd has achieved over the years—helping people to reach higher in their business and personal lives. This book belongs in any professional's business library."

—BARBARA SANFILIPPO, CSP, CPAE
Author of *Dream Big! What's the Best That Can Happen?*
Speaker/Consultant

"*High Trust Selling* turns a job into a vocation. If you want to establish your permanent place in this industry and make a fortune in the process, you better pick up a copy of Todd Duncan's wonderful guide to building customers for life."

—DANIELLE KENNEDY
Author of *Seven Figure Selling* and *Workingmoms.calm*
Sales Trainer, Coach, Consultant

"One of the things we learned when we wrote *The One Minute Manager* is that people can best absorb information . . . and apply it to their lives . . . in small, digestible bites. Todd has done just that in his new book . . . I believe High Trust Selling will become one of the enduring classics of business and personal growth literature."

—KEN BLANCHARD
Author of *The One Minute Manager*®

"This book is required reading for any person or company who is really serious about the business of selling."

—CARA HEIDEN
Executive VP, Wells Fargo Home Mortgage

"With *High Trust Selling*, I'm seeing a fresh new voice . . . committed to helping people achieve success and personal balance."

—ZIG ZIGLAR

"Todd Duncan is one of those rare individuals who has been able to take the measure of his own success—plus the success of hundreds of others—and translate it into a meaningful set of strategies and tactics. *High Trust Selling* . . . is based on reality, built on experience, and loaded with the kind of advice that will absolutely help people in their quest for success."

—KEVIN SMALL
President, Maximum Impact, Inc.

"I believe that Todd Duncan's new book, *High Trust Selling*, is a model of clarity in the spectrum of sales and sales management. Todd makes it crystal-clear exactly how a sales professional can achieve success and personal balance, not with pie-in-the-sky theories, but with hard-hitting, real-world strategies and tools."

—BRIAN TRACY
Brian Tracy International
Author of *The Power of Clarity*

"Todd has shared his uncommon spark—and drive to succeed—with thousands of sales professionals all over the country, and now he has brought it all together in *High Trust Selling*. A great addition to any executive's library."

—TOM HOPKINS
World renowned Master Sales Trainer

"Todd has distilled more than 2 decades of experience and success into 14 very concise, very powerful and very practical laws that can make people successful beyond their dreams. He just plain delivers the goods . . . and people's personal and financial lives are being tremendously and greatly impacted."

—JOHN MAXWELL
Author of *The 21 Irrefutable Laws of Leadership*

When you have done all you can do and can't do any more—your only option is to *become* more. The principles outlined in *High Trust Selling* can equip you to become more than you are today. What you desire to become *can* begin today.

—KAREN FORD
Independent National Sales Director

HIGH TRUST
SELLING

HIGH TRUST SELLING

MAKE MORE MONEY IN LESS TIME WITH LESS STRESS

TODD M. DUNCAN

OLIVER
NELSON™

THOMAS NELSON PUBLISHERS®
Nashville

A Division of Thomas Nelson, Inc.
www.ThomasNelson.com

Published in Nashville, Tennessee, by Thomas Nelson, Inc.

Library of Congress Cataloging-in-Publication Data

Duncan, Todd, 1957–
    High trust selling : make more money, in less time, with less stress / Todd M. Duncan.
        p. cm.
    ISBN 0-7852-6393-4 (hardcover)
    1. Selling. I. Title.
    HF5438.25.D863 2002
    658.85—dc21   2002014844

Printed in the United States of America

05 06 07 08 QW 16 15 14

For Sheryl, my wife

May your life be filled with health and hope.
May your faith and courage lift you higher than your challenges.
And may the joy and peace of trusting God live in your heart forever.

Contents

Foreword xi
Introduction xiii

SECTION 1:
LAYING THE FOUNDATION TO BECOMING A TRUSTWORTHY SALESPERSON   1

CHAPTER 1: The Law of the Iceberg
The Truest Measure of Your Success Is
Invisible to Your Clients   3

CHAPTER 2: The Law of the Summit
Your Direction Is a Result of Your Perception   17

CHAPTER 3: The Law of the Shareholder
Successful Salespeople Buy Stock in Themselves   33

CHAPTER 4: The Law of the Ladder
The Success You Achieve Is Directly Related
to the Steps You Conceive   51

CHAPTER 5: The Law of Leverage
You're Less Likely to Fail When You've Told
Others You Will Succeed   65

CHAPTER 6: The Law of the Hourglass
You Must Make Your Moves Before Your Time Runs Out   79

CHAPTER 7: The Law of the Broom
To Build Your Business Up, You Must First Clean It Up   95

SECTION 2:
Laying the Foundation for Building a Trustworthy Sales Business   113

Chapter 8: The Law of the Dress Rehearsal
Practicing Your Lines Elevates the Level of Your Performance   115

Chapter 9: The Law of the Bull's-Eye
If You Don't Aim for the Best Prospects,
You're Likely to Do Business with Any Prospect   133

Chapter 10: The Law of the Scale
If You Want More Business, Have Fewer Clients   153

Chapter 11: The Law of Courtship
For a Relationship to Be Right on the Outside,
It Must First Be Right on the Inside   167

Chapter 12: The Law of the Hook
A Captivated Audience Stays to the End   189

Chapter 13: The Law of Incubation
The Most Profitable Relationships Mature over Time   211

Chapter 14: The Law of the Encore
The Greater the Performance, the Louder the Applause   231

Acknowledgments   249
About the Author   251

Foreword

by John Maxwell

Todd Duncan's desire to help people discover their purpose and develop their God-given potential is apparent in everything he does, and his latest book is no exception. Over the last few years Todd has become a wonderful friend. We have spent many hours sharing our hopes for our families, vision for our companies, and our goals in life. It is obvious to me that Todd is a great leader, and as you read the pages of this book I know you will also benefit from his leadership insights.

High Trust Selling is not only a reflection of who Todd is, it is a clear portrait of who he desires you, the reader, to become. Todd's words will empower you with the tools necessary to become a great leader in selling. But more than that, they will also compel you to maximize your potential in life. This book can take you to the next level, and I believe it will become one of the cornerstone books for your business as well as the sales industry. Regardless of your current position in the world of sales, *High Trust Selling* is a must-read. But I encourage you to do more than just read this book. Commit to live it.

JOHN C. MAXWELL
New York Times bestselling author of
The 21 Irrefutable Laws of Leadership,
Failing Forward, and
The 17 Indisputable Laws of Teamwork

Introduction

There are millions of sales professionals in the worldwide economic community. And all of them, in one way or another, are striving to be successful. I know from my own studies and twenty-three years of observation that a significant percentage of these men and women will fail. Despite their best efforts, they won't be able to make enough money to support their families. They will become frustrated, burn out, and eventually just quit the sales industry altogether. You may be struggling with these issues right now.

But there is an answer to the dilemma, and you will find it in a unique combination of three common words: *High Trust Selling*. What does that mean?

If you picked up a copy of this book, then clearly you're interested in growing into a more effective salesperson. But I have better news for you: If you are careful to apply the concepts of high trust selling and the fourteen "Laws" described in this book that govern selling success, your sales business will do more than merely improve—it will *explode*. I can say this with a high degree of certainty because I've not only implemented high trust selling in my own career with great success, but I've also seen it work in the lives of thousands of people to whom I've taught it.

Take one of my clients, Steven Marshall. A decade ago, Steven couldn't even see the bar of sales success. This year, he *is* the bar of true success in the sales profession. Ten years ago, Steven sat in the audience at one of my events, merely hoping for a small nugget of wisdom. This year he stands on stage with me, sharing his story and the lessons he's learned with other sales professionals. Ten years ago, Steven was only twenty-one years old, but ambitious. This year, Steven turned thirty-one. He's still ambitious. After all, he still has a lot of life to live. And the truth is that because he follows the principles laid out for you in this book, his business and his life will continue to be more abundant than most salespeople will ever imagine. But hopefully not more abundant than *you* can imagine.

When Steven was introduced to the principles of high trust selling, he was twenty-one and his income was below poverty level. He was a salesperson trying to make it in the dog-eat-dog world of sales with nothing but ambition and a knack for persuasion—and he wasn't making it. He was heavily in debt and his tax returns for the previous year reported an income of about $10,000.

But as he began to immerse himself in the truths of high trust selling and began applying the Laws to his sales efforts, something unexpected began to happen. People began to listen to him more readily. Sales were made more naturally and more often. Success in the sales business was no longer a hope; it became obtainable, and not just monetarily. Yes, his income doubled, then tripled, then quadrupled—and continued to climb. But more than that, a life he never thought possible began to emerge. More money, but with it, more time off. Greater success, but with it, greater significance. His success in sales began to usher in the kind of life he had only dreamed of.

As Steven discovered, sales are made when trust exists. But in the sales profession there's more to steady success than being a trustworthy person—although that's certainly where it starts. *Long-term sales* success happens when *high trust* exists—when you are a trustworthy salesperson running a trustworthy sales business, and when it's clear to your clients that you are a person of integrity who will not only do what you say but who also has the means to deliver. It is one thing to be a trustworthy person with a sales job; it's another to be a trustworthy salesperson with a reliable business.

A trustworthy person will do everything in his power to follow through on what he has promised—and that's very important. But if a trustworthy person is not also an efficient salesperson running an efficient sales business, trust will only go so far. It may land a sale or two, but it rarely will last beyond that. High trust is necessary to climb to the top, whether you're selling cars or copiers; hats or home loans; footwear or financial services. And high trust happens by design, not by accident. It's earned and preserved, but never finagled.

Despite what you've read or been taught to this point in your sales career, it takes more than fortitude and flattery to become great in the sales profession. If you *are* a trustworthy salesperson running a respectable, reliable sales business, you *will* succeed in the sales profession . . . in less time than you think and with much less stress than you're accustomed to. More than that, with high trust on your side you will climb to the top of your industry and remain there.

It was no accident that Steven Marshall attended my seminar in 1992 as a salesperson struggling to make ends meet. And it's no accident that you're reading this book right now, at this point in your sales career. For Steven, my seminar was more than a wake-up call—it was the means for a new life, on and off the job. For you, the principles within this book can be the means to realize *your* dreams, your chance to turn things around, to take your sales to higher and higher levels, and to usher in the life you've only dreamed of.

What Steven learned back in 1992—and continues to apply to his sales business today—is the same truth that you will read in this book. Since 1992, Steven has simply applied the Laws of high trust selling to his approach to sales—and he's reaped the rewards. Within this book are the stories of dozens of salespeople just like you, who through applying the principles of high trust selling have received much more from their jobs and from life than they've ever thought possible.

When I'm speaking at an event, I often look excitedly into the faces of those in the crowd and wonder: *Who's going to be the next Steven Marshall?* It's the same question I ask myself now as I share these selling truths with you, because I know that if you apply what you're about to read, it will change your sales business forever. And more than that, it will change your life. That is my greatest hope for you as we begin. And that, I pray, is your greatest hope too.

SECTION I

LAYING THE FOUNDATION TO BECOMING
A TRUSTWORTHY SALESPERSON

ONE.

The Law of the Iceberg

*The Truest Measure of Your Success
Is Invisible to Your Clients*

Where are you in your sales career? Are you a twenty-year veteran with a few success stories under your belt . . . yet, you rarely feel satisfied with your work? Maybe you've jumped from sales job to sales job, each time hoping things will be better . . . but things aren't better, really. Maybe you've just begun your sales career and want to know how to build the right foundation for your future success . . . but you're not sure where to start. Maybe you're just considering a job as a sales professional and want to know what it's going to take to succeed. Or maybe you're simply tired of mediocre success and are ready for a breakthrough year. After all, every sales professional wants to earn more, in less time, with less stress. Right?

No matter what description best fits your sales career right now, it's never too early or too late to take your success and satisfaction to new heights. And that begins by following the Law of the Iceberg, something Steven Marshall accomplished early in his career.

In January 2000, I received a letter from Steven, and his words spell out the significance of following the Law of the Iceberg:

Todd,

I've been listening to the new Mastery tapes and felt I needed to send you a thank-you note for the unbelievable impact that you and your teaching have had on my personal life.

Obviously, financial increase is the most tangible measurement of success, but I've learned it's not nearly the most important. When

I first attended your seminar in 1992, my income was dismal. My tax returns reported a net income of approximately $10,000—lower than a full-time McDonald's employee. Presently, I earn about $800,000 per year and have over $1.2 million in cash and stocks. I get excited when I think that I went from being heavily in debt to having a personal net worth of over $2 million in just a few years.

To me, however, financial independence is only a small part of success. The true measure of success is being a loving husband and father, being physically fit, being happy and emotionally abundant, and constantly growing and learning. Those are what matter most.

With you as my mentor, coach, and role model, I have defied the odds and set new standards for my career and life. In fact, my life now feels very well-balanced and I have a clear vision for the future. Thanks to you, I feel I have all the resources within me to live my life to the fullest and to realize every one of my dreams. With the momentum I have built, the sky is the limit.

Thank you,
Steven

If every sales professional followed the Law of the Iceberg as Steven Marshall did and still does, there would undoubtedly be less stress, less frustration, less inconsistency, and less dissatisfaction—more motivation, more trust, more money, and more fulfillment in the sales industry. Guaranteed. In fact, whether you're a sales executive, manager, representative, or assistant, understanding and applying the Law of the Iceberg in your sales career is *fundamental* to improving both your finances and your fulfillment. It's vital if your aspiration is greater than merely making a living—if your goal is living your best life.

High trust selling begins for everyone where it did for Steven—by securing your truest measure of success. Because in sales, motives mean everything. Motives dictate your mood, mentality, and moves while serving a client. And motives will make or break you when it comes to establishing loyal, lucrative relationships. The Law of the Iceberg says that the truest measure of your success is invisible to your clients because the majority of real success occurs on the inside of a salesperson, not on the outside. Your fulfillment—not your finances—should dictate whether you are truly successful. "Financial independence," as Steven wrote in his letter, "is only a small part of success."

Put it this way: For you to be a truly satisfied, successful *salesperson*, you must first be a satisfied, successful *person*.

Think of yourself as an iceberg floating in a body of water. Imagine that the part of the iceberg beneath the surface of the water represents what's on your inside: your values, your deepest desires, your mission, and your purpose in life; and the part of the iceberg above the surface of the water represents what's on the outside: your sales position, your earnings, your accolades, and your possessions. Now, if you've ever read anything about icebergs, you know that very little of the mass of an iceberg shows above the surface. In fact, experts estimate that on average only 10 percent of the entire mass of an iceberg appears above the surface. What that means is that 90 percent of the mass is beneath the surface, invisible to those above the water. In other words, what you see above the surface is not an accurate representation of an iceberg at all. It's just the tip. And the same is true of sales success. What's appears on the outside of your sales career doesn't accurately represent how successful you are.

Now imagine what would happen if we could saw off the entire foundation of an iceberg beneath the surface. Without its foundation below the water, what would happen to the iceberg? A dense, substantial iceberg would begin to sink until there was enough of it submerged to regain its balance. It would probably remain standing, but the proverbial tip of the iceberg would be much smaller than it once was. And the iceberg would certainly become much less stable, and much easier for the changing tide to displace.

If a thin, fragile iceberg had its base removed, the tip above the surface would probably fall over. And without a solid foundation, the iceberg would become a slave to the ever-changing ebb and flow of the tide. In fact, without a foundation, the small iceberg may cease to be an iceberg altogether.

In similar fashion, without a solid foundation beneath the surface of your career, your outward success as a sales professional will never

> Most people can discern the difference between a
> salesperson who is out to make a dollar and one who
> is out to make a difference.

be stable or consistent—even if you've been in the industry for some time. Furthermore, you will always have difficulty establishing trust with your clients because you're not trustworthy; your motives aren't right. And most people can discern the difference between a salesperson who is out to make a dollar and one who is out to make a difference. And the longer you try to build your sales career without a proper foundation, the greater the likelihood that your career will come toppling down. You see, true sales success doesn't begin with the stuff on the outside—whom you persuaded last week, how much you sold last month, what you earned last year, or how much you can afford to buy this year. Like an iceberg, what's above the surface is not reliable. Lasting success is built with the stuff on the inside—who you are and who you want to become, why you sell and what legacy you intend to leave.

THE GREATEST INHIBITOR
OF SALES SUCCESS

Let's face it: Many people get into sales in the first place because they want the outward success, the big money, the nicer car, the bigger house. That's how most sales positions are marketed aren't they? "Come work for us and we'll make you rich," is the common sales-position pitch. *A nice base salary with great earning potential. You could make a killing. Oh, and we'll even throw in a few thousand stock options that could yield millions . . . when the company goes public.* I'm sure you've heard that message before.

Now, don't get me wrong. I'm not saying that more money and nicer things are wrong for a sales professional to desire. Who doesn't want those things? As a matter of fact, material increase is a fair reward for being good at what you do. But when you try to build a successful business solely on the basis of attaining such above-the-surface things, your career is likely to share a fate similar to that of the sawed-off iceberg. It will bob up and down, teeter, and eventually sink or tip over.

For over twenty years I have been interviewing, training, and coaching sales professionals, and the one factor I have found that prohibits salespeople from succeeding more than any other single factor is *lack of purpose*. Most haven't answered the "Why?" question for their careers. In other words, the majority of unsatisfied salespeople become that way because their jobs aren't aligned with a greater sense of purpose. And it shows: in their methods of doing business, in their relationships with clients, and on their faces. The problem is that they're trying to build their careers from the outside in. They're looking for inner satisfaction from outward things. But that's backward. And while the desire for money and material things (or anything else inferior to purpose) can keep anyone motivated early on, when the time between sales starts to grow, it's rarely enough to keep one afloat.

Let's be honest. Sales professionals are notoriously gung ho out of the starting gate. We're self-starters, highly motivated, and highly ambitious. But if time wears on and sales grow harder to come by, it becomes increasingly difficult to remain hopeful and excited about what we're doing. And eventually, moving on to something new sounds much more appealing than sticking it out. The problem with this path is that in the sales profession "something new" usually ends up being the same old position selling a new product. And the cycle starts again. Excited. Motivated. Ambitious. Maybe a sale here and there to keep the hope alive. But nothing sticks. Eventually our interest diminishes, and again it's time to move on to something else.

Does that sound all too familiar? Just about every sales professional has taken a lap or two around that track.

But if you've been there, as most of us have, and you want to make sure you don't go there again, I'm here to tell you that there's a remedy for avoiding that circuitous sales career. It's called "pull power," and it's the essence of the Law of the Iceberg.

THE POWER TO PULL YOU THROUGH

If you've never taken time to determine the deeper purpose beneath your sales profession, then your road to high trust selling must start there, beneath the surface, on the inside, before you will ever be truly satisfied and successful on the outside. But once you identify your purpose with regard to success and your sales career and begin to align that purpose with your activities and goals, you create what's called *pull power,* which is the greatest motivating force for the work you perform.

> **To become a successful, trustworthy salesperson**
> **you must first know *why* you want to be one.**

Pull power is the antithesis of willpower, which is merely self-generated energy that produces short-term accomplishment but rarely sustains long-term achievement. To exploit pull power in your career you must know *why* you do what you do. Once established, your answer then becomes the force that literally motivates or pulls you along, in good times and bad, when sales are red-hot and when they're ice-cold. Pull power is your inner accountability, your constant reminder, from the heart, of the deeper reason you are selling. The problem is that most sales professionals get ahead of themselves. Most spend the better part of their early days trying to figure out the "hows" of their jobs. *How can I make more sales? How can I make more money? How will I meet my quota? How can I motivate my sales team to produce more?* They're all questions that have their place. But answering them is not where a successful sales career begins. It's not enough to know *how* to be a good sales professional. To become a successful, trustworthy salesperson you must first know *why* you want to be one.

WHY SALES? WHY ME?

The person who interviewed you for your first sales job probably asked you something like, "Why do you want this job?" Think back. What was your response? Certainly you didn't give a surface answer like, "I want to get rich and buy lots of nice things." You were probably more clever than that, whether or not you really meant it. What would you say if someone asked you that question today? Seriously. Have you ever asked yourself, *Why do I have this job?* Really. If you haven't asked yourself, you need to. Not tomorrow. Not next week. Not when "things slow down." Not after you get your next big account. You need to do it now. And you need to be honest with yourself and ascertain more than a surface answer. You need to get down to the bottom of that question, because if you're just in sales for the money you could potentially make and the things that money could potentially buy, you're probably not going to make it very far. You're certainly not going to weather many rough storms. And if you happen to become one of the few who achieve a measure of success despite never establishing a greater purpose, your so-called success will have come at the expense of your inner satisfaction. I've seen it hundreds of times. Joe Salesperson comes to me after ten years in the business and wonders why, despite his fat bank account and Benz in the garage, he still feels unfulfilled deep down, as though he's missing something. It's a shame. But it doesn't have to happen.

Please don't misread me. I have been the frustrated salesperson. I have lost big accounts, or failed to nail them down. I have gone too long between sales. And I have been Joe Salesperson. In fact, it was at that point in my career—when I had the big bank account, fast car, and nice house—that I finally opened my eyes to the damage I was doing by selling solely to attain outward success.

Those of you that have heard me speak may know that I was a cocaine addict for two years. And over that period of time I spent nearly eighty thousand dollars on the drug du jour. On the outside, I appeared to be very successful, and for that matter, most people probably thought I was satisfied as well. Remember, I was Joe

Salesperson. I had the fat bank account, the Porsche Carrera Cabriolet, the nice place at the beach, custom-made suits, expensive toys, you name it. But the truth is that on the inside I was running on empty, and my destruction was imminent. Fortunately, I pulled myself out of that pit before it was too late. Or to be more precise, my purpose pulled me out.

It began while sitting on my couch after a midnight jog. With cocaine still racing through my veins, my heart refused to slow down. Flipping on the television to try and relax, I watched in discomfort as a television sports anchor announced the sudden death, the cocaine overdose, of a young basketball star named Len Bias. Maybe you remember the terrible tragedy. Here was a young kid, just out of college, who had become the first pick in the NBA draft the day before. He was destined for stardom but his lifestyle caught up with him. The news hit me hard. That night, I finally came to terms with my shortsightedness, and immediately went back to the beginning, to the "whys" of my career, to my higher purpose for becoming a sales professional. And it was there that I found real power to take my career to new heights.

LAYING YOUR FOUNDATION
FOR SELLING SUCCESS

It's pretty straightforward: To follow the Law of the Iceberg, you must be solid on the inside first. You must solidify your higher purpose in your sales career so that you are strong enough to weather the rough tides of the sales profession, focused enough to leverage the best opportunities, and steadfast enough to secure the trust of your clients. With a sound purpose, you establish a firm and powerful foundation for achieving the highest and truest measure of success.

Consider the success of pharmaceutical giant Merck & Company, Inc. In their book, *Lessons from the Top* (New York: Doubleday, 1999, page 144), authors Thomas Neff and James Citrin reported their findings after discussing Merck's last decade of success with the company's President and CEO, Ray Gilmartin. Said Gilmartin:

One of the things [George W. Merck] said was that "medicine is for people, and not for profits. If you remember that, profits will follow." And that's true of my own personal philosophy as well. And the more we have remembered that we are producing medicines to improve people's lives, the more profits we have made. Our share price is a reward for doing that well.

Fortune [magazine] recently ranked Merck as one of the top 10 best companies to work for and in their summary they said that employees like the fact that we are working toward a higher purpose. They spoke to the reporter about our low-cost AIDS drug, which was consciously priced lower than the other protease inhibitors on the market. We could have gotten more money for it, because of the characteristics of the drug. It's something we discussed; but we talked about the George W. Merck philosophy and considered the need of getting the drug to the people who needed it . . . and we came down on the side of the lower price. And I think that not only had a positive impact outside the company but inside as well. This is a very reinforcing concept. So not only do we talk about this stuff about having a higher purpose, but we base our actions on it . . . We're not going to consume our talent or people in the sole pursuit of achieving financial results. We have a higher purpose that we're committed to.

A deeper purpose was, is, and will continue to be the thrust of Merck's success. And of all people, Ray Gilmartin has certainly proven he knows how to succeed in the sales industry. Merck is the largest pharmaceutical company in the world, with revenues in excess of $40 billion and a net income of $6.8 billion last year. Undoubtedly, the consummate success of Merck & Company is a strong case for following the Law of the Iceberg.

LIVING THE LAW OF THE ICEBERG

High trust selling success begins for you in the same place it did for the people of Merck & Company, in the same place it does for every consummate salesperson: by determining your higher purpose in the sales profession.

Your foundational purpose is

> ➤ your core motivation for thought and action in every area of your job
>
> ➤ your deepest inspiration for getting things done
>
> ➤ your critical filter for decision making
>
> ➤ your built-in accountability

Without a foundation of purpose beneath your sales career, you will

> ➤ experience stress
>
> ➤ suffer burnout
>
> ➤ have difficulty making decisions
>
> ➤ put too many things on your plate
>
> ➤ experience inconsistent goal achievement
>
> ➤ suffer defeat by comparison
>
> ➤ feel rushed
>
> ➤ be restless
>
> ➤ feel as if life is slipping by
>
> ➤ lack clarity on what's important
>
> ➤ have a sense that you're missing out

With a foundation of purpose beneath you, you will experience greater

> ➤ passion—more excitement, enthusiasm, and energy
>
> ➤ personal power—more motivation and self-discipline
>
> ➤ success possibility—a better attitude toward selling in general

➤ success probability—a dramatic increase in your odds of succeeding

➤ productivity—maximizing your per-hour opportunities

➤ profitability—higher earnings

➤ predictability—more consistency in your success

➤ persistence—greater willingness to go to the next level

➤ perseverance—more long-term vision to stay in the game and finish strong

There are many ways to determine your purpose at work, but in my experience, the most effective way is to answer one question: *What's important to me about being successful?*

Determining your higher purpose starts with defining the word *success*, because that is the paradigm with which most people identify. But success has many different meanings to many different people. That is why it's important to know what success means to you. Ultimately, the answer to the success question will yield deeper distinctions, stronger motives, and authentic reasons for wanting to be successful—and that's where you discover real power in your pursuits. Dig deep. Don't stop with the first thing that comes to your mind. The deeper you search, the more accurate and more profound the impact of your answer. Here are two examples from my research of how the success question delivers different but equally powerful foundations on which to build one's sales career:

Salesperson A:
Money ⇨ Freedom ⇨ Time ⇨ Making a difference

Salesperson B:
Recognition ⇨ Acceptance ⇨ Excellence ⇨ Adding value

While Salesperson A initially answered that making more money was her definition of success, when she delved deeper beneath the surface she determined that the reason she wants to make more money is that she enjoys the freedom it creates to spend more time with people. After digging still deeper, she discovered that her real motive for spending more time with people is that she wants to make a significant difference in their lives. Bingo. Her definition of success and her wellspring of pull power: making a difference in others' lives. As a result of her discovery, she now enters her office every day knowing that her purpose is to align her actions in such a way so that at the end of the day she will have *made a positive difference* in the lives of the people with whom she's done business—something she has unlimited opportunity for as a sales professional—something that her clients can trust implicitly—something she can achieve independent of financial success.

And while Salesperson B initially thought success meant receiving the recognition of his superiors and peers, he now awakens every day with his mind, energy, and resources focused on giving his very best to his clients so that in the end he has *added value* to their lives—again, a highly trustworthy enterprise—again, a worthy pursuit that can be achieved independent of financial success.

You'll notice that in both examples the salesperson initially defined success in very shallow terms. One said it meant having more money; the other said it meant being recognized for his achievements. Maybe to this point in your career, that's how you've defined success as well. If so, you aren't alone.

But also notice that in both examples, as the salesperson took time to go deeper beneath the surface, each discovered a steadfast foundation on which to build his or her sales career—where each found true power in his or her work. And if you're willing to dive beneath the surface to determine your true purpose in selling, you, too, can build your career upon a rock-solid foundation. As a result, not only will your attitude be changed, but you will also find that a new power is available to you. A power that will not only pull you through the rough waters, but also guide you into client relationships that will spring forth an ocean of true success and fulfillment. And ironically, a power that will even usher in a measure of success above the surface that you haven't seen before. When your foundation beneath the surface is secure, everything above the surface follows suit. Grow beneath the surface and everything above the surface becomes more substantial. That's the Law of the Iceberg. And that's where all high trust selling begins.

SALES LEADERSHIP APPLICATION

Before you can teach your sales team how to apply the Law of the Iceberg, make sure it's solid in your career first. Don't teach something you're not practicing. Once it's a reality inside you, I recommend that you schedule a one-on-one meeting with each salesperson on your team, even if it takes several weeks or months to do so. In the meetings, cast your vision for each salesperson. Describe the steps you took to restructure your career from the inside out and give them tools to do so in their lives. Keep in mind that during this process some of your people may realize that the sales profession is not for them. And while your goal is not to scare anyone off, it will help your people harmonize their careers with their purpose—in or out of sales—giving them the best chance at true success. In doing so, you will not only be setting your team up for success, but you will also be playing out your own purpose as a leader.

CHAPTER

TWO

The Law of the Summit

*Your Direction Is a Result
of Your Perception*

E very sales professional is familiar with failure. In fact, truth be told, we're probably more familiar with failure than success. Even the best. And while many books state that the difference between the successful salesperson and the mediocre one is something like mental tenacity or perseverance, neither is enough to continually motivate us to dial another phone number when the going is really tough. Perseverance keeps you active, yes. Perseverance may even improve your initiative. But perseverance doesn't address the heart of motivation.

One client—we'll call him Dave—is a sales professional who has always been motivated to excel. But that self-motivation is not what helped him more than double his income over the last year. You see, for years Dave attended my events and even hired a sales training coach to help him become more effective and efficient. Certainly he was going down the right track and didn't lack any ambition or enthusiasm. In addition, he's always possessed the tools to be a great high trust sales professional. He is very personable, he's a man of integrity, and he's very thorough. But those things weren't enough. Something was still keeping him from becoming highly successful in his industry. It was his wrong perception of failure.

The truth is that Dave had never really striven for major success because he feared what might result if he didn't succeed. Fortunately, while attending one of my sales teaching events, something inside him finally clicked. He got it. Failure wasn't something to be feared—it was something that was inevitable if he was to attempt big things, if he was to climb to the next level of success. Failure wasn't fun—he knew that. But failure could be very beneficial—even enlightening at times. By the end of the event, Dave found himself excited at the prospect of going about his sales business with a new perspective on failure.

Dave had stopped meeting with his sales coach, who was helping him make the necessary changes in his business approach to improve his results, just prior to my event because he had become disheartened at his marginal success. But after the event he immediately hired a new sales coach. Through the first few meetings with his coach, he discovered that in trying to keep everything under the scope of his control—in an attempt to avoid failure—he had been acting as his own assistant. His initial item of business was to hire an assistant and delegate a large portion of his daily tasks to her. Little did Dave know that this step would become a first chance to test-drive his newly formed perception of failure.

Even though Dave had done a very thorough job of screening, interviewing, and setting expectations with his newly hired assistant, she turned out to be a wrong fit for the job. He was upset—it was a failure, and he felt he had let her down. But with the help of his coach, he learned that the failure had actually helped him better understand the type of person he really needed. Applying this lesson, Dave hired another assistant, this time training her thoroughly on all the ins and outs of his business. And guess what? She liked the business so much, she decided she wanted to pursue a position like his instead of becoming his assistant. This time Dave felt a little betrayed, but nonetheless understood where she was coming from. He let her go to pursue a different position. He knew it was the right thing to do. Once again Dave sought out the lesson in the failed hire, then pulled up his bootstraps and brought on another assistant—his third in a matter of months. And this time he got it right. With the help of his coach, Dave delegated several tasks to his new assistant, freeing up more time to build relationships with prospects and clients.

Today, Dave's perception of failure is right where it needs to be.

While he still doesn't enjoy making mistakes—and who does?—he continually seeks to apply the lessons that every blunder in business is willing to teach him. And if you think that hasn't made a difference in his success, think again. Dave's earnings the year prior to changing his perception of failure were around $200,000. This year he will earn nearly $500,000 and is on pace to become the first salesperson in his company to earn $1 million a year in income next year.

Like Dave, to continue climbing toward higher pinnacles of success, despite past failures and the likelihood of more on the horizon, you need more than stick-to-itiveness. You need more than mental toughness or fervent initiative. You need more than a capacity for psyching yourself up. *You need to be inspired at your core.* When the sky is falling, or has already fallen, you need a foundation to stand on that is more solid than mental elasticity. Bouncing back again and again is admirable; but if that's all you do, your sales career will always feel like jumping on a trampoline. Up and down. Up and down. A lot more activity than productivity, mixed with occasional disorientation and a regular loss of balance. And that's no way to spend your sales career.

> **To continually move from your foundation toward success,
> you must have more than perseverance—
> you must have the right perception of failure.**

To weather the roughest storms, to remain inspired to strive for your summit of success despite setbacks, to maintain the confidence of your best clients, your steps must be established on a steel-strong foundation. And if you remember from the last chapter, the Law of the Iceberg says that your most solid foundation is your purpose, your core definition of success. The Law of the Summit takes this one step further. It says that to continually move from your foundation toward success, you must have more than perseverance—you must have the right perception of failure.

In sales your purpose does more than lay the foundation for your success. With the correct perception of failure, your purpose also acts as your compass, constantly directing and redirecting you toward the summit of success. As a result, failures don't undermine your footing. Missing a meeting with a key partner, being rejected by a potentially valuable client, failing to meet a customer's need, forgetting an important phone call; they all may slow your pace for a time. But such failures should never diminish your motivation, deplete your self-esteem, or destroy your client relationships.

"Failure," rhymed poet William Arthur Ward, "is a delay, but not defeat. It is a temporary detour, not a dead-end street." (John Cook, Editor, *The Book of Positive Quotations*, Fairview Press, Minneapolis, 1997) Salespeople are people, which is to say that we are imperfect like everyone else. You must understand that in order to become proactive with failure. You will fail—there's no doubt about it. And when you accept that fact, you begin to understand that it's not in *ceasing* to fail that a salesperson climbs to the summit of success. Rather, it's in *using* failure to enlighten the path to success.

The truth is that mistakes should never leave you uninspired to continue. In fact, with the right perception of failure, you just might be *more* motivated to sell after a mistake. That's because if you're following the Law of the Summit, a mistake is not perceived as a step backward, but rather a pause for redirection, an opportunity to make a positive change. According to the Law of the Summit, a mistake often offers you a more precise directive toward your summit than any amount of preparation can. And if reaching the summit inspires you, learning how to reach it more effectively is not a disappointing prospect.

The Law of the Summit doesn't suggest that you can simply fail again and again then magically end up successful. It's not that simple; and there's nothing enchanted about it. The Law also does not suggest that when you make a mistake, you call a band, hire a caterer, bake a cake, and celebrate. Let's face it, making mistakes isn't fun. Nobody likes it. In fact, it's usually downright frustrating. But what the Law of the Summit does say is that when you perceive the value inherent in your mistakes, you are able to continually improve your direction toward success with each mistake you make. In other words, with the right perception, failure should make you a stronger climber.

A NEW PERCEPTION OF FAILURE

Contrary to what you might think, high trust selling is not a matter of avoiding mistakes. The success journey is strewn with failure. Furthermore, maintaining a thriving, trustworthy business is not necessarily a matter of failing less than others. In fact, usually, the most successful people have failed more than most. To advance toward the summit of sales success and establish a business worthy of any client's trust, you must recognize the positive role that failure plays in your climb.

When I speak to sales professionals, I usually ask a question that elicits a wave of nervous giggles followed by a large showing of hands. The question: How many of you experience "call reluctance"? Just about every sales professional who spends time on the phone—and that's most of us, because that's where most sales start—has experienced a level of call reluctance. And if you don't know what I'm talking about, try picking a random phone number from the Yellow Pages, then attempting to sell that person on the other end of the number your product. Call reluctance is that feeling you'll get as soon as you begin to dial the number. Why are you reluctant? Because your approach to selling breeds distrust—and you know it. Most people aren't gullible enough to give their hard-earned money to someone they've never met, let alone someone in whom they have no preestablished trust.

Simply put, call reluctance is the natural inclination to avoid the prospect of rejection; and in this particular example it means not wanting to call a person who has no prior reason to trust you, then try to talk him into buying something he may not even need. It's easy to see why so many salespeople are reluctant to pick up the phone every day, isn't it?

Now, you might be thinking, *Cold calling is a thing of the past. Most calls nowadays are to preestablished leads.* And while the sales profession has done well to mask the practice of cold calling by referring to lists as preestablished leads, the truth is that call reluctance still exists even when calling on leads, whether they're given to you or established on your own. That's because you still hear "No" more often than "Yes," and your mind is preprogrammed to shun the "No" calls as much as possible.

Think outside of the sales profession for a moment. In fact, think outside of business altogether and you'll find that our minds tend to react to the potential of rejection the same way no matter what the situation.

Consider the realm of dating. I don't think there is a person on the planet who hasn't felt some sense of reluctance on a blind date. After all, here are two people who've never met about to be thrown together for a couple of hours with the lofty expectations of their friends that something will "click." But things usually don't click, do they? There are moments of silence as both stare at their food or admire the decor of the restaurant. There are uncomfortable instances where his sarcasm is mistaken for rigid doctrine. There are times where he laughs at something about which she was entirely serious. There's that uneasy feeling that one might spill a drink or drop a fork or shoot a meatball off a plate. And then there's the pressure that both feel to keep the conversation going—that ongoing burden to delve deep within their minds and come up with yet another witty or thought-provoking question.

Of course, sometimes blind dates have happy endings—but more often they end with both parties wishing they had never begun. And that's why most people don't like blind dates. The potential for failure is higher than normal. Even with the most optimistic attitude, blind dates breed reticence, inhibition. And it's the same in the sales profession.

If you're still trying to sell with the mind-set that mental tenacity or an optimistic attitude will get you through unpleasant times, you'll always be stuck with a feeling of reluctance. That's because whether you like it or not your mind will naturally remind you of your past failures. Especially if you never learned from them.

Call reluctance is based on the fear of failure. But no matter what you do, you will make imperfect sales calls. People will turn you down. You will botch meetings with potential clients. You will forget things. You will mess up. We're all imperfect people. We all fail. And in the sales profession, the prospect of failure isn't low. While there are certainly proactive ways to improve your manner and methods of selling to increase the likelihood of trust being established (which we will discuss in the coming chapters), the only way to address the issue of failure is to change your perspective. You can try to fail less often; but that usually causes you to endeavor for less-lofty goals, or ones that don't require much risk.

However, when you're climbing for your summit of success, you will enlist the risk of failure. There's no way around it. And the only way to combat failure is to decide to see it as an opportunity to improve your direction. An opportunity to make the call or the meeting or the presentation better the next time around. An opportunity to establish a more authentic trust with your next clients.

If you think about it, that's one of the best ways to improve, right? By learning from your own failures. And despite what you might think about the most successful people in your field, no one does things perfectly the first time. Rarely does anyone have it down on the second, or even the third, try. In fact, the truth of the matter is that the most successful sales professionals spend their entire careers improving little by little with each step they climb. High trust selling is a constant work-in-progress, a career-long process of improvement. And that's how the best salespeople reach the summit, again and again.

A NEW PSYCHOLOGY OF SUCCESS

Before we discuss how to become a peak performer in the sales profession today, it's important that we define the "summit." Many salespeople make the mistake of seeing external things as the summit of success. Sure, successful salespeople earn the money to afford nice things, but external things are not what they see as the peak of their profession. External things such as money, accolades, and awards are perks of success; but having them doesn't mean you've reached the peak. Top-notch salespeople view the summit of success through a totally different lens. In fact, their summit is on an entirely different mountain.

The greatest salespeople see the summit of success as a product of continually improving, continually honing the tools of their trade, continually raising the bar in their chosen field. In fact, when successful salespeople aren't improving, they're not succeeding.

It's easy to be average. It's much easier to stand still than climb. It's also much easier to climb down than climb up. Just don't improve over the course of your career. Try to avoid any prospect of failure. Become an expert at doing things the way you've always done them. It's more comfortable. Or better yet, keep doing what the majority is doing. Make calls the same way. Approach potential clients the same way. Make presentations the same way. Then simply pass off all your troubles and frustrations as occupational hazards, just part of the dog-eat-dog world of sales.

If that's your mind-set, you'll never reach the summit of sales success because you have an obstructed view. Your current distance from the summit is not measured by the amount of money in your bank account. It can't be seen with the eyes in your head. Your distance from the summit is measured by how far you've climbed since your last sale, or missed sale. And sometimes your biggest ascents come on the heels of your biggest mistakes.

> **Reaching the summit of success in the sales profession is not so much what you receive from climbing as it is what you become by climbing.**

Think of it this way: Reaching the summit of success in the sales profession is not so much what you receive from climbing as it is what you become by climbing. You learned in the first chapter that true success comes as a result of being fulfilled on the inside (beneath the surface), not on the outside (above the surface). Therefore, reaching the summit of success is a matter of continually increasing your level of inner fulfillment and satisfaction from your performance. In other words, when you reach one summit of sales success, another higher summit comes into view, and so on. In fact, there is no limit to the amount of summits you can reach in your sales career. While it's true that you can decide to stop climbing at any time, the highest achievers never stop climbing. They are always challenged to continually improve. To take trust to higher and higher levels. As they see it, where there still exists failure, there still exists room to climb. And as a result of this mind-set, their success never ceases to elevate.

BECOMING A WORLD-CLASS CLIMBER

If anyone knows how to perform at peak levels, it's Jamie Clarke, whose summit of Mount Everest in 1997 is detailed in the extraordinary biographical film, *Above All Else*. From age twelve, Clarke dreamed of climbing Everest. His desire and determination eventually led him to the ominous mountain on three different occasions in attempts to reach its peak. The first attempt, however, was unsuccessful. He and his team of climbers were forced to abort their climb 3,000 feet from the summit due to 200-kilometer-per-hour winds. Unfortunately, winter had begun to set in early, and to ensure their survival they were forced to begin their descent without reaching the peak.

Clarke's second attempt failed when his lead climber became too fatigued to meet the challenge of climbing the last 162 meters—the equivalent of just two city blocks. Imagine the frustration as the team again was forced back to the base camp for the second time without reaching the summit.

Clarke, however, wasn't plagued with disappointment. Ironically, he became more inspired to reach the peak than ever before. In his book *The Power of Passion* he shares how he acknowledged that each of his previous climbs were successful because they taught him specific ways to improve. He reasoned that he had come just two city blocks from the summit in his previous climb. He knew that if he was careful to listen to the instruction of his past attempts, his boyhood dream would become a reality. He was, as he saw it, just 162 meters away. Inspired by the lessons of his previous attempts, Clarke immediately set to the task of planning his third mission. And this time his efforts took him to the top.

At 7:10 A.M. on May 23, 1997, Jamie Clarke stood on the summit of Mount Everest, becoming the ninth Canadian ever to reach its peak. For forty-five minutes, he and his team of climbers enjoyed the realization of his dream, the culmination of over eight years of effort. But Clarke understood one thing to be true: Their real success was not in reaching the peak, but rather in the process it took to get there. Moved by the words of Sir Edmond Hillary, who said, "Everest is never conquered, [but] occasionally it does allow momentary success," Clarke wisely noted, "Real winning has nothing to do with standing on the top. Winning isn't anything external at all. It is an internal satisfaction, a deep inner sense of pride and joy" (John Cook, Editor, *The Book of Positive Quotations,* Fairview Press, Minneapolis, 1997).

> **Reaching any peak in life is a result of continually improving, which is often a result of learning from failures.**

Jamie Clarke understands that being a peak performer in any endeavor has nothing to do with the acclaim, money, or awards that might come as a result. Reaching any peak in life is a result of continually improving, which is often a result of learning from failures. And even after the Mount Everest of your career is climbed, there are still other summits to be reached. In fact, Clarke's summit of Everest was just another in a lifetime of peak performances. Consider his achievements leading up to Everest:

➢ published journalist

➢ radio broadcaster

➢ three-time Canadian cross-country ski champion

➢ explorer of over forty countries

And since his summit of Everest, Clarke has continued his pursuit of greater peaks. Not only has he written two books and produced three films, he and his expedition team also put together a peak performance that most say was more perilous than climbing Everest. Turning from the cold and vertical world of the Himalayas, Clarke directed his passion to the most desolate and dangerous desert in the world, Arabia's Empty Quarter. And on March 12, 1999, he and his team completed a 620-mile camel crossing of the scorched and barren land, becoming the first Westerners in fifty years to accomplish the feat. It's easy to see that for author, producer, speaker, adventurer, and explorer Jamie Clarke, there will always be another summit to reach. And so it is with every peak performer.

GOING UP?

Imagine your sales career as a mountain you must climb. Reaching up the mountain is a rope that will take you to your next summit of sales success. Grabbing hold of the rope is a choice you must make every day. When you choose to improve by learning from your mistakes, you choose to grab the rope. And each time you do this, you are more readily enabled to climb to a higher level of success, and eventually to the summit. Now, you can try to climb the mountain without the help of the rope, without learning from your mistakes, but the climb will often be treacherous, unstable, and much more difficult. In fact, often it will be impossible for you to climb at all. And here's why.

Trailing down the mountain is another rope that leads back to base camp, where you started as a sales professional. However, the difference between this rope and the previous one is that the rope going down the mountain is always attached to you. You can't choose to pick it up or set it down. It remains tied around your waist throughout your climb. The reason is because the downhill rope represents the path you've taken since becoming a sales professional. As is the case, the rope passes over every rock, under every tree, and through every river that you've traversed in your climb.

But here's the significance of this rope. When you are careful to learn from each of your mistakes along the way, the rope only remains as an encouraging reminder of the obstacles you've overcome to get where you are. But when you do not learn from your mistakes, the rope gets caught up. Your past mistakes become like a tree root that snags the rope or a crevasse between two rocks that pinches the rope and won't let go. And until you go back and release the rope from its snag, you will have great difficulty climbing any higher. The rope may stretch a little, and you might be able to change your direction to increase the slack, but you won't be climbing up the mountain. Eventually you'll come to a place where your climb will simply become a game of tug-of-war with your unlearned mistakes. You'll be trying to pull yourself up the mountain while your mistakes keep you anchored down.

Which direction are you climbing? Are you ascending toward the next summit by continually learning from your failures? Or are you trying to avoid the prospect of failure by not climbing at all? Maybe you are trying to climb, but because you haven't learned from failures, you're still stuck somewhere near base camp. No matter what direction you've been headed or where you are on the mountain of your sales career right now, you can begin today putting the Law of the Summit to work in your life by adopting the following three outlooks on failure.

1. Failure is OK. Every salesperson fails. The greatest salespeople, the peak performers in your field, are probably the ones who've made the biggest mistakes. But what sets peak performers apart from the rest is that they have learned to not let the fear of failure keep them from attempting to climb. As successful salespeople see it, a wrong step is simply an investment in the success of their next attempts. A failed trust is a lesson in how to more effectively earn trust. See your mistakes that way, and you'll never stop investing in your success.

2. Failure is an advocate. The greatest salespeople know that failure is often their greatest instructor. And with this knowledge, they are quick to look for the lessons in each mistake, be it a glaring blunder or an unseen slip. Failure, as successful salespeople see it, is one of their greatest advocates for success. In fact, without failure there wouldn't be peak performances. When you adopt this outlook on failure, you'll find that there is something you can improve almost every day.

3. Failure is a strong force that can compel you to climb higher. Have you ever lost a game that you know you could have won? How did you react? Did you just stew in your anger and frustration? Probably not. You were probably eager to do something about it, especially if you know how you could have won. Former tennis great Chris Evert Lloyd once said, "If I win several tournaments in a row, I get so confident I'm in a cloud. A loss gets me eager again." With the right perception of failure, you're able to turn your mistakes into motivation, your irritations into inspiration. The reality is that just about every kind of mistake is frustrating. But what's been done is done. And no amount of sulking will change the past. However, you can change the future by deciding to let your mistakes motivate you to try harder and better the next time around. That's the outlook that will compel you to continually reach your summit of sales success.

HIGH TRUST AND FAILURE

Contrary to what you might think, making mistakes doesn't disqualify a person from the trust of another. Trust, in its most primitive form, is based on authenticity, not flawlessness. And while the Law of the Summit does not build a case that mistakes help build trust, it does

> **Trust, in its most primitive form,
> is based on authenticity, not flawlessness.**

indicate that trust can be more greatly solidified with a proper perception of failure.

There is no doubt that you've lost the trust of a client or two, especially if you've been in sales for many years. But what did you do as a result of that broken trust? Did you go out and try to gain trust the same way as before? If you did, it's highly likely that you made the same mistake with the new client. And if that didn't happen, or hasn't happened yet, your relationship with that client is probably functional, but not highly productive. To establish high trust client relationships that last a lifetime, you must be willing to learn from your mistakes. Plain and simple. You may take some knocks out of the sales starting gate while you're learning how to build trust the right way. But over time, by purposing to not repeat mistakes that hindered or broke trust with clients in the past, you will become very effective at earning and maintaining trust the right way. And when trust with clients continually reaches higher levels, so does your success. That's what it means to follow the Law of the Summit.

SALES LEADERSHIP APPLICATION

As a leader it's your job to set the proactive and reactive tone for your company with regard to failure. Your reaction to your employees' mistakes, whether you like it or not, will shape how they perceive failure on the job. Make a point to clearly communicate to your people the inherent value in their mistakes. Help them perceive failure as an advocate to not only their personal progress but the progress of the organization as well. Be big enough to admit your own mistakes when they occur, and share past mistakes that have taught you valuable lessons. Without making light of your team's mistakes, make sure your people understand that failure is OK as long as they improve from it as a result. If you aren't already doing so, make time to meet with your people on a regular basis to "debrief" them on both their successes and their mistakes. Train them to look for the lessons in failure by asking them what they've learned; then give them the freedom to try again with a new understanding and greater inspiration.

The Law of the Shareholder

Successful Salespeople Buy
Stock in Themselves

T im was doing OK, really. He'd been selling for a few years and had managed to rack up $7 million in sales that particular year. But the truth was that he hadn't even scratched the surface of his potential, and he knew it. Then something happened that changed everything. Here's how he tells the story:

> I was jogging one day after work in 1994, trying to release some tension that had built up as a result of some frustrations at work. Then a voice inside me spoke. I can still hear the words as if they were whispered to me yesterday. They basically told me that I needed to stop thinking of myself as an employee of someone else's company and start treating my job as if it was Tim Braheem, Inc., with me as the CEO.
>
> The mind-set that resulted from that epiphany was profound. It changed every aspect of how I did business: the way I marketed myself, the way I valued my clients, the way I cherished my loyal assistants and staff personnel, and, more important than anything, the way I viewed my life and its potential. That day I made a silent declaration that I could one day earn a seven-figure income. It was an infusion of the entrepreneur spirit into my career that lifted the lid off of any limitations that I was placing upon myself by thinking like an employee.

In the twelve months that followed, Tim added $10 million in sales. The following year his sales climbed to $46 million. The year after that his sales reached $75 million. And last year his sales topped $175 million. How did he do it? He determined his answer to one very important question. The million-dollar question that dramatically boosted Tim's business is the same question that can boost yours: *Am I a salesperson in business, or am I a business owner making sales?*

SUCCESS IS YOUR BUSINESS

It makes no difference where you are in your sales career, whether you're a sales manager, sales broker, or sales rep. The million-dollar question applies to everyone in the sales profession. And more than likely, it doesn't matter what company you work for or what product you sell. The fact is, you will not reach your potential as a sales professional until you answer the question, and answer it correctly. The Law of the Shareholder demands that you do.

Over the last seven years my company's coaching partner, Building Champions, has coached thousands of sales professionals to greater levels of success. And in almost every circumstance, the first business breakthrough occurred when the salesperson adopted something I call a "CEO mind-set," which is the point at which one begins to see herself or himself as a business owner who's making sales. It's that simple change in thinking that becomes the catalyst for each salesperson's climb toward greater success. And that simple change in thinking can jump-start your sales career as well.

The Law of the Shareholder says that the most successful salespeople buy stock in themselves. That begins when you stop thinking of yourself as an employee with a job and start thinking of yourself as an owner of a business with a compelling vision to help people. Consider how your thinking has affected your investments in your sales career to this point.

When it comes to your sales job, ask yourself these questions:

> ➤ Do you only spend money on the things that your employer will allow you to expense? *A business owner*

34

would invest whatever is necessary to allow the business to thrive, even if that means using his or her own cash.

➤ Do you simply stay busy so the time passes more quickly each day? *A business owner seizes every minute of the workday because wasted time equals wasted money and wasted opportunities.*

➤ Are you more concerned with your effort or your effectiveness? *A business owner measures effectiveness first—sprinting on a treadmill gets one nowhere.*

➤ Are you more concerned with the quantity or the quality of your sales? *A business owner focuses on quality, knowing that trust established with clients multiplies quantity of sales.*

➤ Are you more concerned with your activity or your results? *A business owner measures results on a regular basis to determine what activities are and are not working.*

➤ Are you more concerned with earning potential clients' cash or confidence? *A business owner knows that without trust she will never realize the full monetary value of a client, and therefore is willing to trade commission for constancy if necessary.*

After reading the questions, would you say you've been thinking more like an employee or a CEO?

The defining characteristic of a CEO mind-set is thinking like an owner. It is taking responsibility for your own growth and the growth of your business. It's understanding that what you do as a salesperson is operate a business that provides products and services, and to do that well and with integrity increases the likelihood of your success and stability. It's knowing that you must have a business plan to succeed. It's knowing that you must have accountability, a "board of directors," to help you make wise decisions that will grow your business. Simply put, it's acknowledging that you alone are the largest shareholder in your business.

> **The life each of us lives is the life within the limits
> of our own thinking.**

Thomas Dreier said, "The life each of us lives is the life within the limits of our own thinking" (John Cook, Editor, *The Book of Positive Quotations,* Fairview Press, Minneapolis, 1997). And that certainly includes your sales career. In fact, the salesperson who follows the Law of the Shareholder knows that to elevate his career, to establish the lasting trust of his clients, he must first expand the limits of his thinking.

A CONTRAST IN THINKING

There's an obvious disparity between salespeople who've adopted a CEO mind-set and those who assume the mind-set of the majority. Here are several examples of how this contrast in thinking plays out in the world of sales.

Salesperson thinking	CEO thinking
Pays only for what can be reimbursed	Invests money to make money
Calls on anybody	Calls on the right body
Reacts to interruptions	Makes sure interruptions don't occur
Keeps safe clients	Terminates unprofitable relationships
Is busy and action oriented	Is productive and results focused
Thinks quantity is more important than quality	Knows quality creates more quantity

Puts profits before people	Puts people before profits
Puts revenue before reputation	Puts reputation before revenue
Builds business ahead of capacity	Builds capacity ahead of business
Prioritizes schedules	Schedules priorities
Is short-term oriented	Is long-term oriented
Relies on quick turnaround	Relies on clients' trust
Succeeds by accident	Succeeds by design

I want to paint this picture very clearly for you because it is so critical. Thinking like a CEO is the first key to understanding the Law of the Shareholder, and it is vital for establishing the long-term trust of your clients. A salesperson who understands the Law of the Shareholder knows that

> ➤ how you work where you are matters more than where you work
>
> ➤ how you sell what you have matters more than what you have to sell
>
> ➤ how you make your calls matters more than how many calls you make
>
> ➤ how many hours you produce matters more than how many hours you work
>
> ➤ getting loyal business matters more than how much business you get
>
> ➤ having clients with high trust matters more than how many clients you have

The future of your sales career rests primarily not in your hands or your feet, but in your mind. In other words, how you think as a sales professional will determine how you act as a sales professional. And until you begin to think like a successful business owner—until you know the statements above to be true—you won't consistently make decisions or take actions that maximize your sales business. In fact, that's why the Law of the Shareholder is the third law. Successful thinking precedes successful acting. And trustworthiness precedes trust. Think about it this way: Until you can think for yourself, customers won't trust your thinking.

The Law of the Shareholder is more than self-affirmation and self-confidence. While you must first think your way to the top before you can ever climb there, mere thinking won't take your sales career anywhere. Like any business, you must actively invest in your sales business for it to grow.

YOUR BUSINESS AS A START-UP

What would you do if you were given the reins to a new business with tons of potential? Think about it. What steps would you take to ensure your success? Well, the first thing you'd probably do is celebrate—it's not every day you get an opportunity like that, right? (And maybe you felt the same sense of excitement when you were hired for your current sales job.) But after the confetti settled, what actions would you take to build a strong foundation for your new business? What would your first priorities be?

I don't think you'd argue that securing some growth capital would be a top priority. After all, you have to invest money to make money. What would come next? You'd probably look for a key person or two to help you run the day-to-day operations of your business, to make sure important meetings were scheduled, important tasks were completed, important phone calls were made, and top priorities were always kept at the top so that time and dollar were maximized each day. You'd probably also acquire some key partners, professionals like yourself who understand what it takes to succeed and are willing to help you make the critical decisions that will keep the company on the upward slope.

Think with me now: What else would you do? There's probably

one more fundamental step that any successful professional would take if given control of a new business. He or she would seek to learn, study, and grow on a personal level. Of course, right? You'd have to invest some time and money in personal growth, not only to stay on top of all the demands of running a business, but also to stay ahead of the competition. To be the leader in your field you'd have to become and remain more competent, innovative, and attractive than your competition. And you'd most certainly have to be able to understand and meet your potential clients' needs better than anyone else.

Now, here's where this gets a little personal. How many of those same steps have you taken for your current sales business? Have you invested capital dollars—your own or someone else's—in the future of your business? Have you hired a capable assistant whose work can help ensure that your time is invested in the things that will bring your business the greatest profit? Have you enlisted the accountability of a few trustworthy advisors to help you make wise decisions and remain on the path to greater success? Do you have a plan for personal growth? If you are a business owner, these are the fundamental investments you must make to succeed. And if you've been trying to succeed without them, I guarantee that your business is not growing at the pace it could be. But the good news is that regardless of your current sales standing, the Law of the Shareholder ensures that when you begin to buy stock in yourself, when you begin to build a business in which people can put their confidence, others will begin to buy stock in you and your business will reap the benefits. Jean's story is a testimony to this truth.

Jean Dees began her second stint as a sales professional in 1992, at the age of fifty-four. She had some success in the sales industry previously, but it had been eleven years since she had called on a client and even longer since she'd had to build a sales business from scratch. But she missed adding value to people's lives. She missed the very things that make the sales profession a privilege. Therefore, she was up for the challenge.

Initially, Jean went about things the way most ambitious,

hardworking salespeople do—she put in a lot of hours trying to max-imize the few resources she had at her discretion to build her new business. She would work fifty-plus hours each week marketing her business, calling on prospects, and attempting to build relationships with clients, all according to the limited resources her employer offered. And while she met with some success, it wasn't enough. Eventually, she sensed there was a better way to go about it. She sensed that she needed to think outside the confines of her current resources. Later that same year Jean invested the time to attend my Sales Mastery seminar in Palm Springs, California. There she learned the important truths of the Law of the Shareholder, namely that she wasn't investing in the right things. The business would come, she learned, when she learned to become a better investor.

Jean had already taken one step in the right direction by attend-ing the seminar. That was her first wise investment. Her next invest-ment was immediately hiring a coach to help her develop an effective business plan that was in tune with her life plan. Together with her coach she determined what additional investments were necessary right away and on a regular basis to reap the business and life she desired. Coaching, they determined, would be a lifetime investment. So would attending personal- and professional-growth seminars. Together with some personal monetary investments and a few initial time investments, these investments got Jean on the right track. She was committed to following the Law of the Shareholder, and before long she began to reap the rewards.

Last year, at the age of sixty-three, Jean received my company's "Lifetime Mastery Achievement Award," which is given to the one sales professional who, year after year, consistently exemplifies excellence, top-notch productivity, and value-added service to her clients. But as Jean would tell you, that's not nearly the greatest return on her investments over the years. Today she, along with her son and two other partners, owns a mortgage company. That allows her the freedom to spend only thirty hours a week in the office, leaving plenty of time for her growing family. In fact, in recent years, her sales business has become a family affair. Her son is now the company president, her daughter a top salesperson, and her granddaughter an intern for the company, spending time with her grandmother while learning the disciplines that have made her a highly successful and satisfied sales professional.

THE TOP TEN INVESTMENTS YOU CAN MAKE IN YOUR FUTURE

Jean's success began with a small investment of time—but over time her investments have reaped a life she could only have imagined. As it was with some of Jean's investments, the returns from following the Law of the Shareholder will often take some time to mature. While there will be immediate returns, such as better organization, less stress, and a greater sense of purpose, the long-term benefits are sure to come: more loyal clients, more free time, more income, and more life. In fact, the longer you stay with your wise investments, the greater the benefits will be.

As Jean's story illustrates, the long-term returns of following the Law of the Shareholder are much more than vacations and cash in your pocket. The returns can be even more substantial and significant. When you invest in yourself and in your business as the Law of the Shareholder teaches, you reap a new life—a more abundant life than you had before, maybe than you've ever had. The Law of the Shareholder isn't just about investing in your business for your business's sake. It's about more than that. Following the Law of the Shareholder is about investing in your business the right way so that your business doesn't run your life. It's about becoming a trustworthy business owner—figuratively and literally—so you can reap a trustworthy business. And in the end, it's about sowing into your business so that you can reap more business *and* more life.

With that in mind, the following are the ten best investments you can make to reap a more secure and successful sales business, as well as a more abundant life. Follow them as Jean did, and you'll reap a very similar reward.

1. Invest in your relationships with those you love. What will your sales success mean to you if you cannot share it with those you love? Don't make the mistake of pushing away those most important to you in the name of "building your business." Your investment of time in your family and close friends is paramount to your sense of fulfillment and success. In fact, your investment of time in your sales business should be in large part to free up more time to be with those you love. Sow into your business to reap more life. Yes, you will reap more business as well. But if that's all you reap, you'll end up a rich salesperson living an impoverished life.

2. Invest in a long-term personal-development program. *You* are your business's greatest asset. Earning a customer's trust begins with who you are. And the growth of your business will always be proportionate to your ability to maximize your personal potential. Are you a good leader? Invest in becoming a great leader. Are you good at building relationships? Invest in becoming great at building relationships so that they're lifelong. Put it this way: Remain as you are, and your business will never flourish. Grow yourself, give people grounds to trust you, and you will be able to grow your business. Grow yourself on a regular basis and your business will remain on the upward slope.

If you want to be a great salesperson who earns trust with confidence then you have to become an expert in your field. One book doesn't do it. A twelve-month subscription to a magazine doesn't do it. Even one seminar every year isn't enough. The greatest sales professionals do all these and more on a regular basis. If you want to reach your selling potential, our research shows that you need a minimum of the following:

Comprehensive training—This gives you a foundation to build from. All salespeople need to start with at least one seminar or similar training regimen that teaches them an effective, comprehensive selling plan. An A-to-Z "boot camp" on how to sell. For you, this book may be your boot camp, and it will be a great start.

Monthly Mentoring—Picking one or two mentors whose tapes, videos, and books will help you maintain focus on the sales plans and disciplines that you must implement and master to continually improve.

Sales Resources—Listening to tapes or CDs, reading sales magazines, and utilizing the latest on-line sales tools on a weekly basis are the vitamins that will keep your growth curve on the up-and-up.

3. **Invest in a sales coach.** You will never know all you need to know to make every decision that arises from running a business. To succeed in sales, you must remain teachable. Therefore, it is imperative that you surround yourself with a competent, trustworthy coach who can help you wade through the muddy waters to see with clarity what is best. And don't make the mistake of thinking that a coach becomes obsolete once you reach a certain level of success. On the contrary, a coach becomes an even greater asset as you climb to higher levels of success, because as the saying goes, the bigger you are, the harder you fall. The more successful you are, the greater your clients' expectations become. Breaking trust is more costly at higher altitudes. But like a skilled climbing partner, a coach helps ensure your falls are never fatal.

4. **Invest in a competent right-hand assistant.** More than likely, you are overqualified for the majority of the tasks you perform. That's because, if you're like most salespeople, you try to do it all yourself. And it's understandable since most salespeople are go-getters. But to run a business effectively, you cannot do it all. You must learn to delegate effectively. And that starts by investing in a capable, competent assistant. Now, you're probably thinking: *I can't afford to hire an assistant.* But remember that we're talking about investing here, not spending. The real question you must consider is, can you afford to not have an assistant?

The fact is that you will never be able to climb to the next level until you free up more time to do what brings your business the greatest profit; and in sales that means building lasting relationships. The more time you have to spend on profitable tasks, the greater your profits can be. In most cases, a well-trained assistant will free up a minimum of four more hours every day (more on this in Chapter 6). That's an additional twenty hours over a five-day work-week—the equivalent of two additional workdays without having to spend seven days a week in the office. And if your priorities are in order, those extra hours can literally earn you ten times your monetary investment.

5. Invest in your personal image. What image are you sending to your customers? If you have a place of business, what impression do people have of you when they walk through the door? What impression do people get when they view your marketing material? What impression does your appearance give? I don't want you to misunderstand what I'm trying to say here: Superior actions can occasionally override a negative or indifferent impression. But more often than not, if your image is not friendly, professional, and inviting, you may never get a sales opportunity with an individual. And such an impression certainly doesn't breed trust.

A negative or uninviting personal image can become a hurdle that customers must overcome before they commit to doing business with you. To avoid this hurdle, invest in items that will improve your personal image, such as top-quality marketing and follow-up pieces, new office furniture, and nice clothing. Keep in mind that until you've done business with an individual, your personal image may be all he or she has to go on.

6. Invest in a personal financial plan. The long-term success of your sales business depends on your ability to reinvest money wisely while maintaining financial growth. That's a given for any enduring business. But let me take it one step further. Your long-term satisfaction with your sales career depends in part on your ability to maintain financial stability. What happens all too often is that salespeople find themselves over their heads in debt, because each time they landed a big account they took on more financial responsibility by purchasing the latest car, house, boat, or you name it, instead of paying off debts. In such circumstances, selling often becomes a hasty necessity of meeting financial deadlines rather than building a profitable business with purposeful, loyal relationships.

Before you get caught in that trap, invest in a meeting with a qualified, trustworthy financial advisor who can help you map out a path to financial stability and freedom. Not only will a financial plan help you reduce the stress of personal day-to-day finances, but it will also allow you to predetermine an amount to be reinvested in your business each month so that your lifestyle can remain consistent.

Let's face it, one of the reasons you're in the sales business is to make money—and one of the reasons you're reading this book is to make more money and eventually to be financially independent. And according to the Law of the Iceberg, that's not a destructive aspiration as long as it's not your main aspiration. So commit to spending some dollars on creating a financial plan that will give you a clear path to your desired financial future and secure your stability as you build your business. Believe me, as a business owner, it's far more expensive not to do so.

7. Invest time in an exercise program. Your career longevity begins with your health. It's a fact that the state of your body can dramatically affect your business, especially in the sales profession. Unfortunately, it has become the norm in sales to work sixty, seventy, or even eighty hours a week. And while you may earn good money doing so, very few last long at that rate. Your body cannot take that kind of abuse, and before long it will tell you so with such ailments as chronic fatigue, chronic anxiety, insomnia, ulcers, headaches, or even a heart attack. I doubt you'd argue that it's difficult to enjoy the fruits of your labor—not to mention life itself—when you're always run-down. The fact is that if you seek a long, successful, satisfying sales career, you must invest in your body.

8. Invest in a client-retention program. To be a successful owner of a sales business you must do more than provide customer service; you must produce client loyalty. That's what high trust selling is all about. Investing in a program that ensures that those with whom you do business always return for more is the greatest dollar-for-dollar investment you can make in your business. I recommend that you focus your investment dollars on four items: creative marketing tools, innovative follow-up procedures, value-added gifts, and client feedback, all of which help to create clients for life. And that is the type of client you should desire most, because their lifetime value to your business will always outweigh any investment you make.

If you own a car dealership, for example, a client-for-life is worth more than $300,000 to the business. If you sell real estate, a client-for-life can deposit more than $80,000 in commissions into your bank account over a twenty-year period through repeat and referral business. When you understand the tremendous value of retaining clients for the long haul, it's easy to justify the investment in their trust up front.

9. Invest in a library. The person you become tomorrow has a lot to do with the books you read today. It may not seem important to invest in books, but you must understand that you will never learn enough through your own experience to out-think your competition. Therefore, you must find another way of increasing your knowledge, and the most effective way is through the lessons of others in books. Your investment in a library is going one step further than investing in a personal-growth plan, because by building a library you will not only provide for your own growth, but will also promote the learning of those on your team—and even your clients—both now and in the future. I have read over eight hundred

---

**The person you become tomorrow
has a lot to do with the books you read today.**

---

books in the last twelve years and am convinced that this commitment to gaining knowledge has helped me to succeed.

10. Invest in technology. This goes without saying if you run an Internet-only sales business. But I am referring here to those of us who conduct business on a face-to-face or phone-call basis. To best meet your current and future clients' needs you must stay up to speed with technology. Most, if not all, of your clients and potential clients have E-mail and Internet access. Therefore, it makes business sense that you utilize those mediums of communication to stay in touch with clients and to promote and conduct business. If you haven't already, consider investing in a Web site for your business that will act as both a marketing tool and resource pool for your clients. Investment #5 comes into play here. Don't invest in a Web site if you're not going to do it right. The appearance and usefulness of your Web site will affect, either positively or negatively, the impressions of clients. If your sales business is done largely through face-to-face or phone interaction, make a point to use your Web site less for marketing and more for assisting and empowering your clients. This will help convey your commitment to people before profits.

YOU CAN PROBABLY AFFORD MORE THAN YOU THINK

The Law of the Shareholder reveals that you must invest regularly in yourself and your business if you're ever going to be successful in the sales profession. That means you don't wait for your company to invest in your sales future; you make the sacrifice yourself because it is your business, and its growth is your responsibility.

As you begin to consider how you should initially invest in the future of your business, I recommend that you assume a new perspective on affordability. One that often has a way of revealing that you truly can afford more than you think.

One of my speaking partners, Tim Broadhurst, has always determined his investment capacity by taking on the following perspective. Instead of looking at his bank account and determining what he can afford financially, he first looks at what his business can't afford to be without, then finds a way to invest in acquiring whatever that is. Like all successful salespeople, he is always willing to invest a minimum of 10 percent of his income goal back into his business. Sometimes, however, it's much more than that.

For example, at an early juncture in his sales career, Tim came to the realization that he was spending too much valuable time performing administrative tasks like making copies, answering the phone, sifting through E-mails, filing paperwork, and buying supplies. They were things that needed to get done, but spending his time on them was not productive, and he was losing sales. He knew that he should have been spending that time on building lasting relationships. But instead of going to his company and asking for an assistant—something for which he knew he wouldn't get approval—he hired an assistant with his own dollars, banking on the fact that the increased time to build relationships would bring a much greater return than he currently produced. And he was right. Over a short period of time the investment proved to dramatically increase Tim's production. In fact his numbers increased so much that his company agreed to pay his assistant's salary after just six months. A wise investment? Absolutely. It's that willingness and savvy to make wise investments in the future of his business that has allowed Tim to build a $100 million-a-year sales business.

Your investments will generate similar returns if you are careful to determine what your business truly needs to succeed right now. Be wise. But also be assertive. You may need to make some tough financial decisions in order to afford the necessary investments. But that's how you run a successful business. You eliminate the hindrances to your progress and integrate catalysts for present and future success. That's the essence of the Law of the Shareholder.

SALES LEADERSHIP APPLICATION

If you are the leader of a sales organization, it is your job to provide opportunities for your people to grow on a regular basis. If you haven't already, commit to putting each of your people on a personal-growth plan that is designed specifically to hone his or her strengths and improve any areas of weakness. Make sure, however, that when you consider each one's weaknesses you only seek to develop areas that will better that individual personally or corporately. Don't try to make the person someone else. The goal in developing your people is twofold: (1) to improve them as individuals and help them live out the purposes for which they feel they are designed, and (2) to improve their value to their teammates, the business, and the business's clients. By adding this kind of value to your team, you will help—not hinder—their efforts to gain the high trust of your customers.

FOUR

The Law of the Ladder

*The Success You Achieve Is Directly Related
to the Steps You Conceive*

There's no doubt that most sales professionals would like their businesses to be more consistent and stable. Then why is it that a large majority of salespeople still squeak by in a maze of inconsistencies? One of the biggest reasons is because they fail to plan for sales success.

In over fifty thousand interviews conducted by my company, less than 2 percent of salespeople admit to having a business plan that they use as a daily guide. And only 10 percent follow a disciplined selling process to ensure a higher probability of establishing trust with customers. What do you think happens when you combine an undisciplined sales process with no plan? For starters, you have neither consistency nor stability in your career. Closing sales becomes a betting game, a roll of the dice. And earning the trust of customers becomes a "right place, right time" kind of thing. Needless to say, you will never build a highly profitable business on that sort of notion.

When Ian McDonald developed a plan, his business tripled the following year. In fact, he produced more sales in the first three months than he did the entire year before.

Ian had been a sales professional for about two-and-a-half years prior to attending one of my events in November 2000. It was there that he realized the critical value of creating an effective business plan. But he didn't realize how *much* value it would add both to his business and his way of life. One month after attending my seminar, Ian met with his new coach and for the first time mapped out a plan for increasing his productivity.

The plan included: expanding his team; forming solid, strategic partnerships; closely monitoring and meeting the needs of his existing clients; advancing prospecting methods; improving overall communication; and drafting an ideal flowchart to indicate how each sale should happen. Then, with his plan mapped out, Ian set his goal at $35 million in sales for the following year. The prior year he had produced $22 million in sales; so he felt $35 million would be quite a stretch, especially considering that his business is conducted in Hutchinson, Minnesota—a town of only thirteen thousand people.

But Ian quickly found out that in fact he hadn't set his sights high enough. In less than four months after implementing his business plan, he had already exceeded his sales goal of $35 million. And when 2001 had come to a close he had produced $66 million in sales, nearly twice his goal, and three times the previous year's total. Oh, and there's something else I forgot to mention—Ian is only in the office four days a week. In fact, his business plan has been so effective that his annual sales goal is no longer monetary. His goal is now to simply conduct business so efficiently that he and his team have a vastly improved quality of life—working only the hours that are required to complete their jobs with excellence, having ample time for their friends and families, and taking vacations when they want to. That's what a business plan is supposed to do—increase your productivity by streamlining your activity and thus increasing your (and your clients') quality of life on and off the job.

The fact is that if you don't have an effective, efficient plan for selling, any business you get is accidental.

What about you? Do you have an efficient selling plan in place? The fact is that if you don't have an effective, efficient plan for selling, any business you get is accidental. The trust you receive from customers will be as temporary as their business. When it comes to selling, hope is not a strategy. Sales consistency is not about consistently being in the right place at the right time with the right attitude. It's about being consistent. It's about having integrity. It's about calling when you say you will call and showing up for appointments on time. It's about listening to your customer's needs and genuinely seeking to meet them with your product or service. And in the end, it's about earning and keeping trust. High trust does not happen arbitrarily. But high trust, and therefore, success, can be predictable if you know and follow a selling plan that works. That's where the Law of the Ladder comes in.

THE PEAKS AND VALLEYS OF SELLING

The Law of the Ladder says that the success you achieve is directly related to the steps you conceive. In other words, to achieve lasting, consistent success in your sales career—to avoid the peaks and valleys—you must first conceive a successful plan. You must first determine what steps are necessary to earn and keep the trust of a customer. Even if you've had momentary highs in your sales career, the truth is that without a plan you are still trying to build your business accidentally, and you will certainly never reach your sales potential that way.

Without a plan, you will still make calls at random and try to secure business before establishing trust. You will still say the wrong things to the right people and lose any trust that could have been established. You will still take business without having systems to provide the product or service on time. Without a plan, you will still be reactive rather than proactive; you will still scramble for quick turnarounds rather than securing constant trust. Together, such counterproductive tendencies eventually create a ceiling of conflict over your sales career. And the only way to get relief from bumping your head is to constantly change gears.

The drill goes something like this: You shift into high gear to ramp sales up. Then—because you don't have a plan—you downshift your productivity in order to take care of the sales you made. You produce a lot of sales one week, then scramble to take care of the sales the following week. You go up . . . hit your head . . . come back down . . . go up . . . hit your head . . . come back down. Peaks and valleys. Sound familiar? And here's the real tragedy: In the end you've worked twice as hard for half as much. Think about it. If you only produce sales every other week, over the course of a year you will have worked for fifty-two weeks but *earned* for only twenty-six weeks. In other words, if you made $50,000 last year in a similar scenario, you should have made $100,000. But the good news is that you can easily avoid this counterproductive practice.

The key is to have a plan that generates the right kind of sales—from the right kind of accounts, backed by the right sales process—that produces the maximum revenue for your time.

The key is to have a plan that generates the right kind of sales—from the right kind of accounts, backed by the right sales process—that produces the maximum revenue for your time. That's the essence of the Law of the Ladder. Let me show you how to follow it in your sales career.

SEEING YOUR SUCCESS

At the head of every successful business plan is a vision for an ideal future, both in business and in life. A business plan will not increase your quality of living or selling unless it's in conjunction with your greater sense of purpose. Ultimately, your vision is the filter through which you sift every business decision, from how to make sales to whom to makes sales to. Therefore, to not have a vision for the future you desire is to invite indecision, instability, and inconsistency into your career. Establishing a greater business vision is the first step to following the Law of the Ladder.

When it comes to establishing a vision for the future of your business, your age doesn't matter. It's never too late to reach for your potential. Sales success doesn't discriminate against age. My father's story is testimony to this fact.

In his mid-twenties, he was an accountant for a major oil company. But in his late twenties he began to sense that accounting wasn't his cup of tea. He began to probe his heart to determine the direction he truly desired for his career. As a result, he eventually developed a new vision for his life. At nearly thirty years old, he determined that he was going to become a doctor; and that changed everything he did from that day on. For the next ten years he put steps to his vision by attending all the necessary schooling. Then, approaching his fortieth birthday, he finally began his practice as a radiologist, which he continued until his retirement twenty-five years later.

Once my dad determined his true vision, he was confident in the steps he took from that day forward. Did he still stumble along the way? Of course he did. But the point is that with a clear vision in his mind's eye, he was able to construct and follow an effective plan that eventually guided him to a successful, satisfying career. That's how vision works. And that's how it will work for you.

Can you see your sales career at peak performance? Take a moment to envision what that looks like. How are you spending your days? What do your client relationships look like? What legacy are you leaving with your clients? Describe your financial state. How much are you making at peak performance? What are you doing with the excess? Describe your life. What are you doing with your increased time off? What does your family look like now that you're selling at a peak level? What legacy are you leaving in the lives of your spouse and children? How do your closest friends and family describe you? What about your life is most fulfilling? Describe your retirement years. What are you doing with the bounty of your sales career? With whom are you spending your days? In whom or what are you investing your money? How will others remember you when you're gone?

This is vision stuff. And it's vital to your sales success. You must be clear on what your future looks like if you're ever to make clear choices in your present. In fact, if you're not clear on what your future looks like now, you need to have a summit meeting with yourself. During that time, you should answer the questions asked of you in the preceding paragraph. Trust me on this: When you begin to develop clarity in your future, you become more productive in your present. It doesn't work the other way around.

> When you begin to develop clarity in your future,
> you become more productive in your present.

THE CORE FOUR

When salespeople graduate from one of my events called the High Trust Sales Academy, they have learned that at the core of tremendous growth as a sales professional is a life plan, a business plan, a time plan, and a client plan. These are what we call the Core Four of sales success. Without them, high trust is highly unlikely. With them, the sky's the limit. In fact, it is not uncommon for graduates to see a doubling of both business and free time in the first year of implementation.

While I know that you are probably anxious to take action—and with good reason—an accurate understanding of the Core Four is necessary to lay the groundwork for creating and implementing your high trust selling plans effectively. In the coming chapters, we will discuss the details of how to construct an effective selling plan, but for now, make it your goal to gain a broad, usable understanding of the following four parts that will make up the core of your most effective sales strategy.

For James the process of determining the Core Four didn't begin until he was thirty years old, but it changed his approach to sales entirely—and his approach to life. James entered the computer sales industry straight out of college, and for eight roller-coaster years he'd been using the same so-called "sales strategies" he'd first learned: Lots of aggressive cold calling, lots of finagling, lots of manipulation (something he called "salesmanship"). He'd become comfortable with making cold calls since he made nearly thirty a day. And he'd even become tolerant of rejection since it was, he was told, the norm in the sales industry.

But he'd never felt fulfilled in the sales industry. It was just what he did to pay the bills. Sure, he'd met with some success—he'd been named the "Salesperson of the Month" three times. And when he was twenty-eight, he'd made nearly $50,000 in income—his best year. But there was so much that James was missing, and I'm not just talking about sales and profits. He was missing out on life. For the past three years he'd averaged seventy hours a week in the office or on the road with clients who gave him only sporadic business. He hadn't taken more than three consecutive days of vacation in over four years, and his two small children barely knew him. Clearly something had to change. And that something was the core of his approach to the sales business.

CORE #1: YOUR LIFE PLAN

From the Law of the Iceberg you learned that 90 percent of your success is invisible to your client. What that means with regard to planning is that setting up your career to succeed follows setting up your life to succeed. A sales career cannot be built to endure unless it is founded upon the blueprint of your life plan. Life does not happen when sales are over. Sales happen when life has truly begun. In other words, *to be productive on the job, you have to be productive off the job*. If things are not right in your life, it will eventually upset things in your work.

A life plan is a five-to-eight-page document that details the five ingredients that embody your life:

1. your purpose;
2. your values;
3. your vision for your value areas;
4. your short-term goals for each value area; and
5. your daily activities that will pave the way for greater success and fulfillment in each area.

For most people, sketching a life plan takes a few days—a short span of time, however, in comparison to the years of fulfillment the plan will reap. Many of you may have this information in your head and therefore just need to take a few hours to write it down. If you haven't yet written out your life plan, I highly recommend that you take whatever time you need to do so now. Even if that means putting this book down for a few hours or days until it's completed. Remember that your business plan will not be complete or as fulfilling if it doesn't integrate your life plan.

For James, sketching his life plan was fairly easy—he'd been sure of himself all his life. He knew what was important to him and he'd even gone as far as planning to make some changes "next year" in order to usher in the kind of life he really desired. But next year never came. What wasn't easy for James was the realization that he'd been neglecting the things he valued most: his wife, his two children, his close friends, and his health. The life he truly desired had been passing him by while he was sitting at a desk. It was shocking to realize. But he also recognized that he could do something about it now, while time was still on his side.

CORE #2: YOUR BUSINESS PLAN

An age-old adage says that if you fail to plan, you are planning to fail. Now, I don't believe for a moment that you have become a salesperson to fail. But if you truly want lasting success and satisfaction, you must construct a plan for how your business must be run to achieve high trust sales. I'm not talking about a plan for meeting your quota here. There's obviously value when your plan includes your sales manager's goals for you. But ultimately, the responsibility for success falls squarely on your lap; and it's much more effectual to make plans based on your own expectations than those of another. The fact is that without a business plan of your own, goal setting and time management are shallow hopes that will never fully materialize.

In the very least, a successful business plan embodies your answer to this question: *What do I want my sales business to look like three years from today?* Most salespeople cannot clearly articulate their answer. But here's the deal: If you don't know where you want to be in the future, you will never get there. That's because planning is merely busywork—spinning your wheels—if you don't know where you're going. However, once you establish a three-to-five-year vision for your business that is married to an effective plan, you can then go about the task of setting long- and short-term goals, and most importantly, planning your time.

It didn't take long for James to determine what he wanted his sales business to look like in five years: He wanted to be working forty hours a week or less, experiencing less rejection, making a six-figure income, and adding value to peoples' lives through what he sold. It was a simple vision that he knew would take more clear and specific steps to deploy. But it was where he needed to start in order to clearly map out the details of how the vision would come about.

THE FIVE ESSENTIAL ELEMENTS OF A SUCCESSFUL BUSINESS PLAN

Business plans certainly vary depending on the company and clientele. But my research and experience have led me to conclude that every business plan must include the following five elements to add purpose to your daily activities and regular disciplines. Because each element builds upon the previous one, I call this the Five-Step Ladder to Successful Business Planning. Here are the basics, and you will see the details later on in the book.

Step 1: Determine volume goals. Determining your volume goals involves establishing three things: your annual income goal, your monthly and yearly sales goals, and your conversion goal or the percentage of sales attempts you want to result in closed sales.

Step 2: Determine daily numbers. To determine your daily numbers, you must ascertain the number of sales you must make per day or week in order to meet you volume goals.

Step 3: Establish lead generation and management strategies. With your predetermined daily sales needed and your conversion goal in mind, determine the required number of sales attempts you must make each day to meet your numbers. For example, if you need one sale per day to meet your volume goals, and your conversion rate is typically 25 percent, you will need to make four sales attempts a day.

Step 4: Establish standards for prospects and clients. Your standards must include the following: (1) A minimum monetary return for your investment in a prospect, (2) the minimum number of sales or referrals required per year from current clients, and (3) your necessary actions for establishing high trust with prospects and clients to see that they produce the appropriate number of sales. I'll explain this in detail later.

Step 5: Employ target marketing. By this point in the planning process, you will have determined whether you need more or less clients. I won't go deep on this here other than to say that one of the top disciplines of every effective sales professional is prospecting. In fact, no salesperson can survive without employing an efficient recruiting process that channels prospects into high trust clients-for-life.

CORE #3: YOUR TIME PLAN

Obviously, your business plans radically affect how you use your time. The goal must then become to schedule your daily priorities so that your time on and off the job is maximized. This is an important point to consider. If you have not implemented an effective plan for maximizing your time on the job, you will never be fulfilled off the job. Remember that if things aren't right off the job, they eventually won't be right on the job; and that includes how you spend your time. The truth is that for most salespeople, their greater values are found outside their workplaces, often in their homes. A Time Plan allows you to best exploit your time on the job so that your time off the job is always maximized.

If you have not implemented an effective plan for maximizing your time on the job, you will never be fulfilled off the job.

For graduates of our High Trust Sales Academy, the Time Plan is the most difficult and yet most rewarding part of their sales development. In fact, we've found that most students who master this principle are able to double their business, income, and free time within nine months of fully deploying their plans.

For James, the essence of his Time Plan was simple: Invest the majority of his working hours selling to prospects and clients who had given strong indications that they were satisfied with his product, shared his core values, and desired to pursue a long-term, mutually beneficial relationship.

CORE #4: YOUR CLIENT PLAN

The fourth and final pillar of a successful high trust sales plan is your client plan. As you will learn later in the book, there are four types of clients; two types are worth serving and developing and two are not. The problem is that most salespeople spend their time trying to work with every type of client and end up spending more time selling to clients they shouldn't be and less time selling to clients that warrant all their time. James had been doing this for 8 years and had little success to show for it. But once he determined to invest his time more wisely, it became clear that he needed to begin focusing his resources on prospects and clients who offered a high return for his investment, and to whom he offered tremendous value.

The basis for having a client plan is the understanding that your sales success will always be based in large part on how your clients respond and perform. While most salespeople have been programmed to believe they have no control over this aspect of sales, that couldn't be farther from the truth. In fact, an effective client plan has everything to do with controlling what clients you sell to and what clients you don't. And the process starts before you recruit clients and continues as you establish and foster their trust. While this element of your selling plan is undoubtedly the most overlooked, it is probably the most significant in terms of decreasing your stress because there's nothing more frustrating than trying to earn the trust of someone who is not worth your time.

THE 90-DAY BURN

When you begin to follow the Law of the Ladder in your sales career, you will probably feel the anxiety that often precedes accelerated growth. And that's OK. You can readily use that energy to begin the more difficult work of implementation that is just around the corner. But where this Law is concerned, your job is to first do the work of resolving your Core Four plans—regardless of how hectic your current schedule is. It is very important that you carry this out in a focused, condensed period of time. I like to call this "The 90-Day Burn." It is not so important that it be only ninety days. However, it must be a sustained period of time, generally three to six months, when absolute focus is placed on the initiatives that will cause quantum leaps in your sales business.

One of our students, Penny Doubek, put the Law of the Ladder into practice when she returned to her sales career after having her third child. It had been years since she had been a sales professional; and, although she had achieved sales success, her life had been out of balance, so she sought out direction before she got started again. After attending one of our events, she learned the 90-Day Burn concept and knew such a time was critical if she was to succeed in the sales profession and have a balanced life as wife and mother. With the principles she had learned at the event, she spent September through November of that same year doing a 90-day burn, giving 80 percent of her time to determining her vision, developing her plans, and building her systems. Then, with her plans firmly in place, she let it rip.

And in forty-five days of actual sales, she qualified for her company's President's Club.

Today Penny is a success, producing in excess of $40 million in annual sales. And, most important to her, she is maintaining a balanced life with her family.

To understand the 90-Day Burn concept as Penny did, consider the launching of the space shuttle. When the countdown hits zero, the shuttle goes full throttle and burns approximately 80 percent of its fuel in the first ten minutes of flight. This is necessary for it to get off the ground and beyond earth's atmosphere. Then, once it's free from the restrictions of gravity, the shuttle simply taps its fuel supply for any course corrections it must make while in flight. The same is true for any salesperson who desires to "launch" his or her business. You must focus a majority of your resources into a condensed period of time on the front end to launch your sales career beyond the confines of its current location. But once you do the burn, you will find that your sales career will shift to cruise control, allowing you to enjoy a more abundant, fulfilling life.

Following the Law of the Ladder will initiate your burn—it will ignite the launch of a more successful sales career. Focusing your time and energy to secure your selling plans is like hitting the switch that ignites your engines. And once you burn your resources on developing dynamic plans, it won't be long before your success reaches heights you never thought possible.

SALES LEADERSHIP APPLICATION

As the leader of a sales team, your success is largely dependant on the success of your people. Therefore, one of your primary jobs is to help your people create compelling visions and plans for their own sales careers—to set them up for success. This will increase both their personal productivity and your corporate productivity. It's important, however, that you don't try to cast a vision or create plans for your people, but rather offer them helpful suggestions, guidance, and support when appropriate. And keep in mind that for some salespeople this will be a very difficult task and may take some time to complete. If it makes sense, offer to meet with your people after hours when the demands of the day aren't so heavy on them. This usually allows both of you to speak more candidly and openly, and will also help build a stronger sense of camaraderie among the team.

The Law of Leverage

You're Less Likely to Fail
When You've Told Others You Will Succeed

I n sales, sharing your goals and dreams with the right people can be the difference between average and above-average success. That's because accountability produces the leverage necessary to follow through with your aspirations. The right kind of leverage is much more than motivation or hope; it is the essential link between what you desire and what you do, between your dreams and your destiny. Without leverage, you'll never reach the peak of your potential. In fact, without leverage I probably wouldn't have become a professional speaker.

Back in 1981 my sales manager asked me if I would share some of the secrets of my sales success with the other salespeople in our company. While I was young and still had much to learn, I was committed to using creative approaches to prospecting, had developed a disciplined selling process, and was continually striving for new ways to improve in my presentation skills. So that's what I shared with the others. Before long, I was sharing my tricks of the trade with the people in my company on a regular basis. Then, after a few years and a few success stories from the salespeople with whom I had shared, some coworkers asked if I had ever thought about speaking on sales development professionally. I told them I had not. But that day a seed was planted—one that just needed some leverage to grow.

Fast-forward to 1988. I was now entering my ninth year of professional selling. I had become one of the top salespeople in my company but was still striving to improve. So one day, when an associate asked me if I wanted to join her for a seminar that was being presented by Tom Hopkins, I decided to attend. I figured the information Tom would provide and the networking with other sales professionals qualified the seminar as a good use of my time.

During the morning break of the seminar, I managed to corner Tom Hopkins on his way back to the stage and I told him that I was very inspired by the seminar. Then I said something that changed everything. "Tom," I said, "I want to be a speaker." That was it. The cat was out of the bag.

"Why don't you see me after the seminar is over," Tom replied, "and we can talk about it." I didn't know it then, but that moment a foundation of leverage was laid that would dramatically change my career and my life.

When the seminar ended, about two hundred people quickly lined up to have Tom autograph copies of his new book. As the line shortened in front of me, I realized that several people had lined up behind me. So I stepped out of line and went to the back, not wanting to be rushed when my turn came to talk with him. Finally, it was just the two of us, and as we shook hands Tom looked me in the eyes and said, "So you want to be a speaker, do you?" With confidence I said yes. Then his eyes turned serious and with an earnest tone he asked, "So, when are you going to be one?" I blew it. I wasn't prepared for *that* question. As a result, I blurted out something stupid like, "I don't know." Then, with calm certainty Tom replied, "If you don't know when you are going to be a speaker, you will not do the things today that will help you become one tomorrow." I was both staggered and inspired in that same moment. "Pick a date," he continued, "and put it in your planner. Then write it on the back of your card and give me your card."

Just like that, the hammer had fallen. The moment of truth had arrived. With little certainty I selected a date, wrote it on my business card, and handed it to Tom. He looked down at the date then said, "If you don't call me by this date to tell me you are a speaker, I will call you and ask you why you have not held to the commitment you just made to yourself." That was the Law of Leverage at work in my life.

YOU CAN'T CLIMB ALONE

Leverage ensues when you share your goals with the right people. That's important for you to understand. The people with whom you share your aspirations must be the dream stokers in your life, not the dream soakers. They must be dream makers, not dream breakers. They must be people who have hearts for seeing you succeed and hands for helping you do so. They can be sales managers or spouses, friends or coworkers, mentors or professional coaches. But what's most important is not what roles they normally play. What's most important is that you have confidence that they care about who you are and who you desire to become. You see, leverage is a result of sharing your dreams with people whom you know will help you reach the top. Think of it this way: Following the Law of Leverage is like throwing a rope up the mountain of your career and knowing that people are there who will secure the rope and help pull you up the mountain.

The fact is that you cannot reach the peak of high trust selling by going it alone. No one climbs Everest solo and lives to tell about it. To be successful and satisfied in your sales career, you must surround yourself with people who will push, pull, drag, and drive you to greater heights. People who are willing to make the climb with you. "Good company on the road," as someone once said, "is the shortest cut." My story is testimony to this.

> **To be successful and satisfied in your sales career, you must surround yourself with people who will push, pull, drag, and drive you to greater heights.**

I was three weeks away from the date I had written on my business card some four months earlier when I remembered that Tom had said if I wanted help, to give him call. So that's what I decided I had to do because I wasn't going to make the deadline I had committed to. Reluctantly, I dialed the number of his company's office and was somewhat relieved when Tom's assistant told me he was on the road conducting seminars. She assured me that she would give him the message and that he would try to call me back as soon as he had time. Two days later, I heard my company's receptionist announce over the intercom, "Todd, Tom Hopkins is on line three." More leverage. He was calling me from Atlanta's Hartsfield International Airport, and for the next forty-five minutes he helped me fill in the missing pieces to make my career transition.

After hanging up with Tom, I knew I had to act. And I did. The following Monday I resigned from my sales position and began my profession as a speaker. I still needed help getting to where I wanted to go in my new career, but now I knew where to get that help. I had experienced firsthand the power of leverage and immediately sought to create more. In fact, since my initial conversation with Tom, I have never been without leverage.

What about you? What is keeping you from stepping out and making the changes necessary to climb to the next level? Like me, could it be that you just need a little leverage? The fact remains that without the leverage that was created when I shared my dream with Tom, I would not be where I am today. I may have never made the transition. But I did; and you can make a significant climb too, if you're willing to put the Law of Leverage to work in your career.

LEVERAGING YOUR LIFE

The beauty of leverage is that once it's created, it permeates more than your sales career. Leverage adds tremendous value to your life and to the lives of your clients. As a result of my conversation with Tom Hopkins that day years ago, I ascertained a path toward my destiny—making a difference in people's lives through speaking. With leverage on my side, I was given an opportunity to begin maximizing my gifts and abilities. Was I using my gifts and abilities before I had leverage in my life? Yes. And you may be as well. But I was not tapping into my full potential, nor was I truly fulfilled. There was only so much I could accomplish by myself. In fact, there was only so much I *thought*

I could accomplish. But through Tom's mentoring I realized there was more available for me if I took the correct steps. Leverage not only pointed me in the direction I needed to go, but it also pushed me down that path and kept me on it—the path that I would have continued to dream about but may have otherwise never taken.

To understand the value of leverage, take a look at the following acronym for the word *LEVERAGE*:

Leverage allows you to . . .

Love what you do. Leverage helps you continually invest in the tasks that make sales a pleasure—namely, building and maintaining loyal relationships. And leverage helps you continually avoid the tasks that make sales a chore. The reason is simple: When you travel down your career path with others who know your deepest desires and are committed to helping attain them, those people act as your guides, keeping you on the most productive and promising path. They offer you suitable and steady reminders of why you do what you do. They keep you honest and trustworthy. They help you sell from your heart. In short, they keep you focused on that which brings you both success and fulfillment.

Equip yourself for excellence. As we've already discussed, leverage provides the means to maximize your gifts. It helps you earn trust the right way. While leverage doesn't put the tools in your hands, it certainly places them at your fingertips.

With leverage you are best positioned to follow through on your commitments to personal and professional growth. With leverage you are best positioned to follow through on your commitments to your clients. With leverage you are positioned to receive innovative tips and techniques for improving your selling performance and increasing your sales productivity. In short, with leverage you have the key to every door of opportunity before you. As the saying goes, the future is in your hands—and with leverage you hold the keys.

View yourself as you can be. Leverage expands your thinking and distends your dreams. Like a thermal rising up from a mountaintop, leverage lifts your beliefs to greater heights. And as Kierkegaard declared, "What wine is so sparkling, so fragrant, so intoxicating, as possibility!"

Embrace the change necessary for growth. You must accept that change is inevitable in life and in your career, especially if you want to continue growing. With the right leverage you are much more likely to mark change as a catalyst that not only produces something different but also something better.

While many changes in your sales business are inevitable—the market will change, your clients will change, your approach will change, and even your desires will change—leverage positions you to profit from change when it does occur, unexpectedly or otherwise.

Reach your goals more regularly. Leverage taps into the power of programming. There's no magic formula. With leverage you are simply more mindful of the things you desire to accomplish, and as a result, you tend to be more productive and purposeful with your time. Leverage, in other words, helps you keep your mind's eye focused on your goals so that your actions follow suit.

Analyze what's working and what's not. Every successful salesperson must learn to remove what hinders business and retain what enhances it. Leverage shows you the difference between the two and gives you the tools to constantly create positive change in your business. In fact, to be successful at high trust selling, you must be willing to run your business understanding that what works today may not work tomorrow. Leverage helps you remain teachable so that you can readily adjust accordingly.

Give up to go up. With leverage you can afford to make the big sacrifices necessary to achieve the future you most desire. Leverage allows you to live out the "pay now, play later" principle because it provides you a net of support. Not only that, leverage helps ensure that you do not give up what must be kept, and do not withhold what must be given. While you still must give something up to get something better, with leverage you will never do so at the expense of your most treasured values.

Engage in accountability. "Show me who you frequent," reads a French proverb, "and I will tell you who you are." In other words, the people with whom you associate can make or break you. The right kind of leverage, created through the accountability of those wiser than you, propels you to the peak of your potential. In fact, strategic accountability is the fundamental application of the Law of Leverage.

LEVERAGING YOUR WAY TO HIGHER LEVELS OF SUCCESS

How much leverage would you say you have in your sales career right now? Have you surrounded yourself with trusted advisors with whom you've shared your vision and plans? If you have, then your career has leverage. But if you have yet to enlist the help of others in your sales career, then it's time to allow leverage to push, pull, and propel you down a more successful and fulfilling path.

To best leverage your sales career you must employ it in three areas. Let's look at them.

LEVEL 1: PERSONAL LEVERAGE

Enlisting personal leverage begins when you commit your plans to paper. In other words, recording your goals and dreams is your first act of commitment in following through on them. The last chapter taught you how to do this most effectively. But simply writing your vision, goals, and plans down is not enough to effectively create leverage. You must also commit to review what you've written on a regular basis. Only then are you providing accountability to yourself. In essence, you are regularly reminding yourself of your commitments.

Personal leverage is really just a result of self-discipline. It's acknowledging that merely thinking about your dreams is rarely enough to create the habits necessary to follow through. Personal leverage is acknowledging that thinking your way into acting is much less likely to occur than acting your way into thinking. But for personal leverage to be most effective in your career, you must also give your dreams a date. If Tom Hopkins had simply told me to write my dream to become a professional speaker on the back of my business card, without assigning it a date, I probably would've never followed through. And even if I had, it would have been on a much later date than when I actually did.

> **Thinking about your dreams is rarely enough to create the habits necessary to follow through.**

That fact is that a dream with a deadline provides positive pressure. Dreams with deadlines are blessed burdens. That's because dates make you find a way to follow through, rather than fumbling with excuses. They get the planning process underway whether you like it or not. The problem with many salespeople is not that they don't have lofty aspirations. We've already acknowledged that the majority of sales professionals are go-getters and usually have an abundance of ambition. The problem lies within a salesperson's ability to act on his or her ambition effectively. Assigning a date to a dream that's written down forces you to figure out how to act in an effectual manner to meet your deadline. That's where your plans come into play.

But I'd be lying if I told you that personal leverage is enough to make you successful in the sales profession. It's simply not. While most salespeople are ambitious, we also tend to be very creative when it comes to making excuses. Think of the lines you've spun to potential clients to try and satisfy them. And if you do it with others, chances are very good that you'll wax just as poetic to yourself. The reality is that there is only so much leverage you can create within yourself. While ambition (and creativity) are both important, they will never create enough leverage to get you to the top. To succeed at a higher level, you must create leverage on a higher level.

LEVEL 2: ASSOCIATE LEVERAGE

Your next step in leveraging your sales career occurs on an associate level. It is here where true accountability takes place. It is also on an associate level where you must do the work of recruiting partners who will help your career, not hinder it.

It's one thing to go out and ask a few friends to occasionally inquire if you're doing what you said you would. It's another to enlist people who will help you do so. Creating associate leverage is not about establishing an environment in which you're comfortable. All that does is affirm your current level of success, or lack of success. True associate leverage helps you act beyond your comfort zone so that you continually climb higher, as does the trust of your clients. That's why it's vital that your partners be people who aren't afraid to ask you the hard questions, the questions that stretch your mental capacity to its peak, the questions that elicit actions that challenge you to do more than you are currently doing.

Ed Conarchy, Kevin McGovern, and Don Elbert are three sales professionals who work for the same company. All three strive for sales excellence, and had individually achieved a great level of success. But something extraordinary happened when the three began holding each other accountable.

It was 1996 when the three attended a Sales Mastery event with the CEO of their company. Little did they know that what they were about to learn would, in a matter of a few years, triple their incomes. As they listened to the different principles that were taught at the event, something inside each of them—the power of possibility—began to surface. Each in his own way realized the value that could be added to their businesses and lives if they were to begin to hold each other accountable to reach their goals and maintain higher standards of selling. It seemed to be the one thing that each was missing. Before the event was over, the lesson had manifested itself in the form of some friendly competition. In the process of holding each other accountable for reaching their goals, the three decided they would raise the bar every month by trying to outsell one another. And in the end, they did more than outsell one another—they outsold themselves.

In 1995, the year before the three learned the value of the Law of Leverage, their numbers looked like this:

Ed Conarchy   119 orders, $16.2 million in sales
Kevin McGovern   102 orders, $14.3 million in sales
Don Elbert   132 orders, $15.6 million in sales

In 2001, after six years of competitive accountability, their numbers looked like this:

Ed Conarchy   394 orders/units, $63.4 million in sales
Kevin McGovern   283 orders/units, $45.5 million in sales
Don Elbert   362 orders/units, $57.5 million in sales

Today, the trio accounts for 65 percent of the company's profit. If that's not a strong testimony of the power of the Law of Leverage, I don't know what is. And here's the kicker: They aren't finished. I recently spoke with the CEO of their company, and he believes their numbers will climb even higher because they are so serious about continually taking one another to the next level. And I'm sure he's right because that's precisely what happens when you follow the Law of Leverage.

Like Ed, Kevin, and Don, associate accountability partners might be coworkers for whom you have a great deal of respect and who have a proven track record of high trust selling success. Associate accountability partners might also be people who have proven themselves successful in another profession and whose character qualities you'd like to emulate. One associate partner may be your spouse, who probably knows you better than anyone and who finds a great deal of fulfillment in seeing you succeed. Or they may simply be close friends with whom you grew up or with whom you attend church. But no matter where you find them, the bottom line is that they take your success and satisfaction personally—that they find fulfillment in your fulfillment.

LEVEL 3: PROFESSIONAL LEVERAGE

There is yet another level on which you can create leverage that can provide you with the means to reach the highest level of high trust selling success. And while professional leverage may cost you money out of your own pocket, it will be money well invested.

Professional leverage results when you employ the services of a professional coach or mentor. It is in this type of accountability relationship that your selling skills are best honed and your plans find the most productive path. A professional accountability relationship is the type of relationship I stumbled into when I met Tom Hopkins. Through his wisdom and unexpected generosity, he put wings on my wish to become a professional speaker. Since that day nearly fifteen years ago, I have kept in touch with Tom and have employed the help of several others of his caliber like Zig Ziglar, Brian Tracy, Ken Blanchard, and John Maxwell. With Tom's help and the advice and support of my other mentors and coaches, I've been able to reach a level of success as a speaker that I had only dreamed of before. And they still help me climb now.

But the fact remains that without the help of my professional accountability partners, I would only be looking up at the place I am today. The same is true of you. If you want to climb, and continue climbing, to higher levels of selling success and fulfillment, you must have professional leverage in your career. Like me, don't wait to simply stumble across someone who has a heart to help you. Take initiative to invest (your own money if you have to) in a professional coach or mentor whose goal is to help you bridge the gap between your dreams and destiny.

LEVERAGE BEGINS WITH YOU

I have seen the Law of Leverage in action hundreds of times since my initial conversation with Tom Hopkins. In fact, I now do with a few salespeople what Tom did for me. It's a tremendous privilege and it adds to the fulfillment of my career. And when others come up to me at a speaking event to tell me that they want to do more, be more, and earn more, I always ask them "When?" because my life is a living example of what happens when you follow the Law of Leverage.

If you want to be a better salesperson tomorrow than you are today, you must stop talking about it and start doing something. That starts by following this Law. To this point in the book, we've discussed four Laws that primarily have to do with the right attitude, foundation, and approach to high trust selling. But the Law of Leverage is about taking action. It's about ceasing to sell alone by reaching out to others who will help you succeed on a level far greater than you can by yourself. It's about becoming more vulnerable in accountability relationships so that you can be more valuable in client relationships. It's about multiplying your partners so that you can multiply your propensity for success. It's about leveraging your best sales career . . . so that you can live your best life. That's how the Law of Leverage can work for you. And it begins when you do.

SALES LEADERSHIP APPLICATION

One of the most important roles that you play in the lives of your salespeople is that of a mentor and accountability partner. However, such relationships will not be as effective if you do not have someone who is pouring into you. Accountability is most effective in an organization when, from the top down, each leader has both a mentor investing in him and a "mentoree," a pupil, in whom he is investing.

Your first step as a sales leader is to establish a relationship with a mentor—someone whom you respect and who will pour his or her sales insight and passion into your efforts. Once you have established that relationship, you can effectively invest in the lives of your sales team. When it comes to this step, it's certainly not possible to be a mentor and accountability partner to every one of your people, especially if you head up a large sales team. However, I suggest that if you haven't already, you begin by making yourself available to no more than the top twenty percent of your sales staff. If you have five salespeople under you, this means you will only invest to this level in one. If you have fifty people on your sales team, this means investing deeper in the lives of ten.

Obviously the more people you invest in, the less time you will have to give to each, so use your discernment when determining how many people to invest in—especially if you have a sales staff larger than fifty people. Keep in mind that your overall strategy in doing so should be to invest on a deeper level with a small number of key people who will in turn agree to develop and equip a small number of key people beneath them.

It's not possible for you to personally reach every person on your staff directly; but through effective, ongoing accountability and mentoring, you can indirectly reach the young leaders on your sales team and develop them to excel at higher levels.

CHAPTER

SIX

The Law of the Hourglass

You Must Make Your Moves
Before Your Time Runs Out

I t's your turn. The pressure is on. The sand in the hourglass is falling fast. Your mind is racing, trying to determine your next move. Even if it is just a game, you don't like to lose. And right now the game hangs in the balance. The outcome, however, is still in your hands. If you make your move—the right move—before the last grain falls through the narrow passage of the hourglass, your team has its best chance of coming out on top. But unfortunately, you're a little sloppy. You're not mindful of the time, and the last grain falls to the bottom of the hourglass before you can advance. Now the outcome of the game belongs to someone else, one of the other players who is just as eager to win.

Have you ever played this kind of game? Take Pictionary, for example. Your turn requires you to draw a picture of a specific person, place, thing, or action before all the sand falls through the small hourglass. If your teammates identify your drawing correctly in the given allotment of time, your team advances. But if the time runs out before you can produce an identifiable drawing, you aren't allowed to advance. And what's worse, the other team then takes control of the game. If you've ever played Pictionary, which most of us have, what are your tendencies when you're the one drawing against the clock? Aren't you keenly aware of the sand falling through the hourglass? Doesn't your pace quicken when you realize that your time is running short? I doubt you play nonchalantly as though you have all the time in the world. It's not likely that you are surprised when your time runs

79

out. The truth is that in board games like Pictionary most of us are very aware of the falling sand. Because you know that in any timed game, if you aren't mindful of the clock, you're more likely to lose than win—even if you're the most talented player. You know that if you can't produce your best effort in the right amount of time, then your acumen and abilities don't matter.

Let me ask you another question: How do you play the game of sales? Are you ever mindful of the ticking of the clock? Do you use your time efficiently, and regularly meet your deadlines? Or are you mostly unaware of how your time is spent and frustrated that you never seem to have enough time to make your best moves?

In the game of sales, if you're not keenly aware of the falling sand, of how you're spending your minutes, you are most certainly wasting your ability, and more importantly, your client's time. And you're probably not winning nearly as often as you could.

MANAGING YOUR MOVES, NOT YOUR TIME

The Law of the Hourglass is simple to understand. It says that to win at the game of sales, to make more sales than you lose, to earn more trust than you break, you must learn to exploit the sands of time. This is true every day. Unfortunately, most salespeople don't follow this Law. Time runs out on most salespeople every day, before they've made the right moves, before they've done what's necessary to earn a client's trust. And what results are shallow, short-term sales, if any sales at all. While you might blame your boss for overloading your plate, or your assistant for not keeping you in the loop, or your clients for dragging their feet, the truth is that you are the only one to blame. It is you that determines your own fate with the moves you make or don't make. It is you that is ultimately responsible for how the game of sales is played. It's when you fail to wisely utilize the time you've been given that the game is played out on someone else's terms, with an arbitrary set of rules that you cannot control.

Years ago, when Walt Disney asked Mike Vance to think of ways to increase the gross revenues at Disneyland, he wasn't sure where to start. He knew that Walt was a man who prided himself in the effective use of time in everything he sought to accomplish. He knew that Walt had a unique understanding of the intrinsic value of time and constantly studied and experimented with techniques to maximize the use of his time to achieve a myriad of goals. In fact, the term "Think out of the box" was coined to describe Walt Disney's way of thinking. Mike knew that he, too, had to think out of the box by employing a deep respect for time as the foundation for what would be done to increase productivity.

The seed of an idea came when Walt and Mike sat down to dinner with R. Buckminster Fuller, famed inventor of the geodesic dome. At one point during dinner, Fuller explained the meaning of a term he coined called the "Ephemeralization Principle" which in laymen's terms means maximizing the use of time by getting more productivity from less time. He used the example of Henry Ford's invention of the modern assembly line, which produced more with less labor and essentially ushered in the industrial revolution.

With a fuller understanding of maximizing the use of time, Mike sat down with his team of creative thinkers at Disney and began to examine ways they could increase gross revenues. They made a survey of Disneyland activities day by day, hour by hour, since it had opened. And they made a discovery about the park's ineffective use of time— Disneyland was only open five days a week, and on three of those days it was only open for half of the day. Mike and his team knew that this was an inefficiency that needed to be remedied if Disneyland was to continue to be a success. We'll talk more about their strategy later in the chapter.

In the game of sales, your turn comes many times in a given day. The most successful and satisfied salespeople learn to consistently make the right moves to secure the right relationships in the right amount of time. But when you consider that the time allotted to each sales professional is the same—twenty-four hours in each day—you must conclude that the most successful salespeople do something more than merely manage their time.

Truthfully, you can no more effectively manage the time during the day than you can the sand in an impervious hourglass. High trust selling requires something more than time management.

"Time management" in its purest definition is an attempt to bring order to something that by nature cannot be ordered; an attempt to define something that is indefinite.

All successful sales professionals understand that you cannot control the standard of time. You cannot stop the sand from falling through the hourglass. Time proceeds consistently and constantly, whether you like it or not. And when it's gone, it's gone.

I don't bring this to your attention to discount all the books and articles that have been written about managing your time. Time management does, after all, have value in that it often creates an awareness of how and where time is wasted. But time management alone is not sufficient. It's one thing to more greatly value the time you've been given, but it's another to exploit it in the best means possible. And the latter only happens when you learn to manage the moves you make.

Top-performing sales professionals who achieve the high trust of their clients consistently don't attempt to manage their time. Instead they manage the moves they make each day. They do this by forming a circular strategy that ensures that each move they make is connected to both their preceding and succeeding moves. In other words, like a consummate chess player, they know that victory demands that every move they make builds momentum for the next move.

Salespeople who follow the Law of the Hourglass are purposeful about their moves each day. They seek out every possible use of their time and make sure none is being wasted or going untapped. Mike Vance helped Disney do this, and the enormous success of Disneyland is the result.

When Mike and his team of creative thinkers took a look at the survey of how Disneyland's hours were used, they quickly saw an opportunity to improve. At the time, Disneyland was closed every Monday and Tuesday, and on Wednesdays, Thursdays, and Saturdays it was only open for half-days. The challenge that Mike and his team faced was to utilize the time that Disneyland was closed to produce revenue. As they saw it, that time was only being wasted because no one had put enough thought into how to exploit it. They had assumed that people wouldn't use the park during that time. But they were wrong. Filling that time to produce more revenue became their aim.

The first step was to come up with a way to get people to the park on the days (Monday and Tuesday) or evenings (Wednesday, Thursday, and Saturday) that it was usually closed. They started by going through the Yellow Pages to stimulate ideas. When they got to C, someone shouted, "Let's start a club!"

"We already have the Mickey Mouse Club," a naysayer exclaimed. Nevertheless, the idea stuck and the team continued on that train of thought. If you became a member of this new club, they determined, you could attend Disneyland on club nights at a discount and enjoy special programs. They decided to call the new venture the Magic Kingdom Club, and it eventually generated enough popularity to open the park every day.

The next step came as a result of someone taking a look at the hours that Disneyland was to be open each day: 8:00 A.M. to 12:00 A.M. What about those eight hours between midnight and 8:00 A.M., someone wondered? They wracked their brains trying to think of ways to use that time. Then someone came up with the idea to ask schools if their students would be interested in using the park during those hours. Young kids, they figured, would enjoy the late hours and exclusive use of the park. As a result, a high-school principal was asked if there was any way to get his school to the park at 3:00 in the morning. He responded with a unique proposal that would begin a long tradition in schools around the world. "Let me have my grad nights at Disneyland," he replied. And so the Disneyland grad-night tradition was initiated, again increasing revenues at little cost.

What Mike Vance and his team did for Disneyland, you must do for your sales business. Are you exploiting all of your time? Are there minutes or even hours that are being wasted each day? Take an honest look at how you're using your time. It's a fact that the most successful salespeople appropriate more profit from a twenty-four-hour portion of time than their peers. One trustworthy move leads to another trustworthy move. One successful action leads to another successful action. Instead of spending time trying to re-create momen-tum day in and day out, top-notch salespeople roll out an effective strategy that will maintain positive momentum which leads to increased productivity. In short, they figure out how to get on a roll and then stay on it.

WHAT'S AN HOUR WORTH TO YOU?

In Chapter 4, one of the things that the Law of the Ladder should have taught you is that to be a highly successful salesperson you must envision your goals for the future of your business. And one of those goals has to do with your sales volume over specific time periods: yearly, monthly, weekly, and daily. A foundational significance in determining your volume goals is that you learn the necessity of valu-ing your time to effectively reach your goals. The Law of the Ladder helps you become more purposeful about the steps you take each day. The Law of the Hourglass takes this one step further by teaching you to assign a specific value on each hour that you spend on the job. Let me explain.

Professionals from lawyers to mechanics to computer technicians to graphic designers know the value of an hour's worth of work. And so do you if you hire one of them. Why? Because the value of each of their services is quantified with an hourly rate. For example, when you hire a mechanic to put a new transmission in your car, you're paying not only for the part but also for the number of hours that the car must be serviced. And as we all know, the longer the work takes, the more expensive the service becomes. In fact, in many cases the cost for the service is higher than the cost for the parts. That's because a mechanic's time is more valuable than the parts he sells. A mechanic understands that without his time, a transmission doesn't have much value to you.

And therein lies the beauty in this exchange (if you're the mechanic, that is). If the mechanic—who, let's say, is the best in town—wants to charge you $100 an hour for his time, he can. Because without him you just have a transmission and a car that won't drive—two things that do you no good if you don't know how to install a transmission.

Of course, it's your prerogative to take your business elsewhere, to another mechanic whose work isn't as good. But if you want first-class work, it's going to cost you $100 an hour, because that's what the mechanic has determined his time is worth. Will the mechanic work on your car for less? No, because there are always other people with car troubles who will agree to the value he has placed on his time—especially people who've used his services before. The bottom line is that he doesn't do cheap work because his time is more valuable than that.

Now think about your job. How valuable is *your* time? Would your clients say that the time you give them is more valuable than the product you provide? Do you work as though your time is more valuable than your product? As a salesperson, you must ascertain the value of an hour of your time if you're ever going to learn to exploit the clock effectively. Now, I'm not suggesting that you begin charging clients by the hour for your time. But what I am telling you is that to be a highly proficient salesperson you really should establish the value of an hour of your time and, like the mechanic or lawyer, refuse to work for anything less. That's what it takes to follow the Law of the Hourglass effectively.

The value that you assign to an hour of your time is initially a goal until you measure your progress in the weeks and months to come. But your hourly rate is easy to figure out once you've determined your volume and income goals. Let's say you determined that your goal over the next year is to net $96,000 in profit from sales. That means that you must net $8,000 a month, or $2,000 a week, or $400 a day. If you plan on working ten-hour days to launch your business to the next level, the value of one hour of your time is therefore equal to $40. That hourly rate then becomes the measurement by which you control the employment of your time—what you do and with whom you work.

Your hourly rate is not only a measurement of how well you are using your time but also an indicator of your trend toward a more profitable future. If you don't know your hourly rate, you're probably losing money every minute. If you don't know the value of your hours,

> **Your hourly rate is not only a measurement of how well you are using your time but also an indicator of your trend toward a more profitable future.**

you'll spend days on things that aren't valuable; and you'll produce things that aren't productive. But when you frame your working days with a predetermined hourly rate that complements both your business and life plans, you will begin to maximize the twenty-four hours you've been given each day. You will begin to win the game of sales from your competitors on a regular basis because your moves will become purposeful, confident, and efficient. And most importantly, you will have time to establish high trust.

When you know the value of an hour of your time, your job is then to never spend time on a task that produces less than you're worth, now or in the future. I will teach you how to master this concept in the next chapter, but for now, let's concentrate on how to best determine what tasks are worth your time.

MAKING YOUR BEST MOVES DURING YOUR BEST MINUTES

Early in my career, I was introduced to what is most commonly called the "80/20 Rule." In the mid 1990s, I stopped teaching this principle because I thought it was too rudimentary. I searched for a more practical and effective principle to describe how to effectively exploit one's time as a salesperson. But over the years—as I continued to study and interview highly successful salespeople—the 80/20 Rule kept coming back to me. I came to recognize that it is not in fact rudimentary, as I had suspected. Rather, it more accurately offers the strongest foundational understanding for effectively determining what tasks are worth your time. An understanding of the 80/20 Rule is fundamental to applying the Law of the Hourglass.

Over the course of my studies, I discovered a wonderful explanation of the 80/20 Rule from Arthur W. Hafner, Ph.D., Dean of

University Libraries at Seaton Hall University. According to Hafner's extensive research, Vilfredo Pareto (1848–1923) was an Italian economist who in 1906 observed that 20 percent of the Italian people owned 80 percent of their country's accumulated wealth. Over time and through application in a variety of environments, this analysis has come to be called "Pareto's Principle," the 80/20 Rule, and the "Vital Few and Trivial Many Rule." Called by whatever name, this mix of 80 percent/20 percent reminds us that the relationship between our output and input is not balanced.

In short, Pareto's rule states that a small number of causes are responsible for a large percentage of the effect. If you're an average salesperson, that means 20 percent of your sales efforts usually generate 80 percent of your sales results. The flip side is that 20 percent of your results absorb 80 percent of your resources. Therefore, to most effectively exploit your time and utilize your resources to execute high trust selling, your job is to distinguish the right 20 percent from the trivial 80 percent—to determine what 20 percent of your efforts and resources are truly "worth" your time.

To help you begin thinking of the areas in which you are not getting your money's worth from your time, the following are some examples of what to assess:

➤ *Business Costs*. To reduce your costs, identify which 20 percent require 80 percent of your resources. If the items that currently fall in this 20 percent are not top profit generators, consider either removing the items from your expenditures altogether or altering your efforts so that you no longer require them in such great supply.

➤ *Personal Productivity*. To maximize personal productivity, start by assuming that 80 percent of your time is spent on trivial activities. Analyze and identify which—if any—of those activities produce value to your sales business and then shift your focus to analyzing the vital few (20 percent) activities that produce the greatest profit. What do you do with the activities that aren't productive? Find a way to either delegate them or simply discontinue spending time on them.

➤ *Product Mix*. If you engage in your own marketing or advertising, you probably engage in some form of market segmentation by identifying groups of people/organizations with shared characteristics and then aggregate the groups into larger market segments. This segmentation may be behavioristic, demographic, geographic, or psychographic.

The 80/20 Rule predicts that 80 percent of the profits in such endeavors will be derived from 20 percent of the segments (or client groups). If your costs are allocated to certain segments and the segments are then rank-ordered by profit, overall profits will increase if you no longer spend marketing time or dollars on the less-profitable segments.

➤ *Profits*. To increase profits, focus your attention on the vital few clients (top 20 percent) by first identifying and ranking your clients in order of profits and then focusing sales activities on them. The 80/20 Rule predicts that 20 percent of your clients yield 80 percent of your profits. Your aim is to determine which 20 percent of your clients yield most of your profits, and spend the majority of your time building high trust relationships with them and those they refer to you.

MORE EXAMPLES OF THE 80/20 RULE

The 80/20 Rule doesn't just apply to profit margins and marketing strategy. When it comes to your time, it applies across the board. Take a look at a few more examples of how the rule plays out in the not-so-obvious areas of your business. If you're not currently following the Law of the Hourglass, it's likely that

➤ 80 percent of your interruptions come from the same 20 percent of the people

- ➤ 80 percent of your problems are a result of the same 20 percent of your issues

- ➤ 80 percent of your advertising results come from 20 percent of your campaign

- ➤ 80 percent of your Web site traffic comes from 20 percent of your pages

- ➤ 80 percent of your customer complaints are about the same 20 percent of your products and/or services

- ➤ 80 percent of your shipments utilize 20 percent of your inventory

- ➤ 80 percent of your decisions made in meetings come from 20 percent of the meeting time

- ➤ 80 percent of your company's annual sales come from 20 percent of the sales force

- ➤ 80 percent of your staff headaches come from 20 percent of your employees

- ➤ 80 percent of your future business will come from 20 percent of your current business

- ➤ 80 percent of your growth will come from 20 percent of your products

- ➤ 80 percent of your success comes from 20 percent of your efforts

It's easy to see from studying these examples of the 80/20 Rule how you can vastly improve your use of time and resources by analyzing the inputs that are required for you to produce the outputs you most desire. Don't throw in the towel if, during your time analysis, you find that you're spending a large majority of your time on tasks that aren't really worth your time. Most salespeople fall in this category. But the fact that you're taking this step now puts the outcome of the game in your hands from this day forward. And as long as you continue to follow the Law of the Hourglass and remain shrewd with your time, you will set yourself up to win the high trust of your clients more often.

Remember that working toward earning your hourly rate every day means analyzing each task that a client or potential client might require of you during the course of your day. Trying to control your day is not enough. Some days, things come up every fifteen minutes that will steal your time if you're not aware of what that time is worth.

THE 100 PERCENT QUESTION

What would your business look like if you could spend 100 percent of your time doing the one or two things that had the greatest impact on your profitability? I am not asking what your sales business would be like if you worked 24/7. I simply want you to start thinking about your time capacity in new terms, with fewer boundaries.

Then I want you to consider how things would be different if you were actually able to spend all of your time doing the few things that you enjoy most and that produce the greatest impact on your business. What would happen to your productivity? What would happen to your cash flow? What would happen to your client relationships? How would your best clients be served better? What would happen to your level of satisfaction? Would you have more time for life? If so, what would you do with that extra free time? How would your life be different? How would it be better?

It is necessary to consider these questions, because your answers aren't far from being reality if you're willing to apply the Law of the Hourglass in your sales business right away. It's not complicated. You see, tantamount to your success is a better approach to productivity: You must begin spending time doing what you do best and delegate or dispose of the rest. The 100 percent question personifies this approach. Focus on doing what you do best for the greatest possible amount of time, and let everything else be handled by a system or a person managing a system on your behalf. Do that and you will win more high trust sales than you lose. Of course, you can continue wasting time doing the things that decrease your hourly rate—but the only way you'll increase your business in that scenario is to increase your hours. And if you're highly ambitious, you've probably already been down that road. Besides, no one really wants to work *more*. That's an inadequate solution.

The truth is, selling is not your life. At least it shouldn't be. But high trust selling can give you more life if you're willing to invest your selling hours wisely—if you're willing to exploit the falling sand the best that you know how so that the outcome of each day remains in your hands. In fact, when you put the Law of the Hourglass into practice, it's highly likely that you'll be spending fewer hours at work while yielding greater benefits. That's how high trust selling is meant to be.

Jane Floyd had been in the sales industry for six years before she realized the amount of time her job had been taking from the things that were most important—namely her family. In 1997, Jane hired a sales coach, and things began to change. Her first item of business: spend three weeks recording everything she spent time on at work. So that's what she did, and she was astounded at the results. Things like spending an average of thirty minutes a day at the fax machine suddenly became more than merely unproductive lulls in the day—they became time away from the things that mattered most to her.

As a mother of two, she realized that two unproductive hours on the job equaled two hours she could not spend with her kids. Motivated to better utilize her time at work, she determined to delegate everything that she didn't physically need to do herself. The process began with delegating typical tasks like making copies, faxing, and filing, but over time evolved to delegating tasks like getting gas in her car and picking up her dry cleaning. Her goal was to become as efficient as possible so that work time would no longer get the best of her—her best time was what she wanted to give to her family and top clients.

Back then, Jane worked an average of sixty hours a week. Today, Jane works about thirty-five hours a week, spending all of her work time doing one thing: building relationships with her clients and strategic partners. And if you're wondering whether her sales business suffered as a result of her cutback in hours on the job, it didn't. In fact, it's quite the contrary. Last year was her most profitable year in the eleven years she's been a sales professional. But while she made more money than any year previous, she'd tell you that was not where she realized her greatest profits. Her greatest profits were realized at home with her family—a result of learning how to follow the Law of the Hourglass at work.

FROM WHY TO HOW

You are unique. And hopefully you've chosen selling as a profession because you feel that you have unique gifts that allow you to not only excel at sales but also to enjoy it. If you don't love selling, then the 100 percent question doesn't work in your sales career because your preference will always be to spend your time doing something that doesn't produce sales. However, if you've read this far, I believe that you probably know you have a God-given ability to sell, that you are now more clear on why you are selling, and that you have an idea of those few things on which you should focus your time and resources to greatly improve your business.

But even if you're not yet clear on how you should be spending your time, don't worry. The rest of the Laws in this book are dedicated to helping you understand and implement the necessary disciplines for becoming highly trustworthy and highly successful in the sales profession—such disciplines as time blocking, prospecting, partnership planning, presentation management, solution marketing and follow-up, and relationship fulfillment.

The purpose of the first six Laws was to help you understand the solid, heartfelt foundation that governs high trust selling success, to give you the right perspective on your life and on success so that you can efficiently shape a satisfying career, to help you understand the "whys" of selling so that you can effectively and immediately implement the "hows." The final eight Laws will teach you how to build a highly trustworthy and thriving sales business. They will teach you how to succeed practically and purposefully so that you produce more than an abundance of high trust sales; you can also produce an abundant life.

So if your foundation is sturdy, let's begin constructing the pillars of perpetual sales success and significance, which starts by following the Law of the Broom.

SALES LEADERSHIP APPLICATION

As the leader of a sales team, your first step to following the Law of the Hourglass is pretty simple. You must evaluate how you are spending your time. If you're not effectively profiting by the clock each day, it affects your ability to lead your people practically and ethically. Practically speaking, the leader who wastes time regularly rarely has any quality time to give his people. In short, poor use of your time undermines your leadership. Ethically speaking, you can't teach what you're not practicing.

On the other hand, if you become effective at following the Law of the Hourglass, you're able to spend your days developing your people and, with integrity, stop spending so much time on tasks that are counterproductive to you and your people. Remember that one of your most important jobs as a sales leader is to develop and equip your people to succeed, which includes teaching them how to order their priorities so that they have optimal opportunity to practice high trust selling. As a leader, it's one of the most important moves you can make.

CHAPTER

SEVEN

The Law of the Broom

To Build Your Business Up,
You Must First Clean It Up

Most salespeople spend only 25 percent of their time selling because they spend 75 percent of their time managing the sales they've made. That's because most salespeople don't understand the value of quality. Quality systems, quality clients, and quality sales produce a quality career. But the problem is that in most schools of sales thought, "quantity" is the highest standard of measurement. As a result, most sales careers are quantity-heavy—how many hours you work, how many units you sell, how many clients you have, and how many calls you make. And in the process, you end up with an unbalanced business practice in which you're only spending 25 percent of your time, or less, actually selling. But the Law of the Broom teaches just the opposite.

The Law of the Broom says that to take your business up to higher and higher levels of trust and effectiveness, you must first clean it up. In essence, the result is taking the unbalanced equation and flipping it around so that you're spending the majority of your time selling.

As I write this, it's been just over a year since business partners Brian Crist and Tres Miller learned the value of applying the Law of the Broom; and they've already seen tremendous results. It was at one of my sales events that Brian and Tres realized how inefficient their business had become. Both had been sales professionals for approximately two years and had managed to survive on their tenacity and sheer determination. But as they listened that day at the event, one of the speakers described how important his own discoveries of inefficiency had been in reaching a higher level of success. When Tres heard this, it hit home. In fact, it was a "Eureka!" moment. He literally slapped himself on the forehead for having missed it, then motioned to Brian that he finally understood what was holding their business back. Brian was in full agreement—it was time to do some sweeping.

For the next four months, the partners cleaned up their sales business beginning with their personnel. Some of their people had displayed an inability or lack of desire to efficiently handle their responsibilities. This had been compounding Brian's and Tres's hours every week, as they had to regularly put out fires that could have been avoided and redo tasks that were carried out in a substandard manner. It was taking from their time to sell, so they let some people go and replaced them with better fits.

Then for their newly formed team, Brian and Tres created fresh job descriptions, making certain that everyone on the team knew exactly what was required of them and was empowered with the tools to excel. Before long the two partners were working in a much cleaner, streamlined environment, which allowed them to delegate the majority of their tasks and focus on what they do best. Today, Brian and Tres spend their days doing what they love—building relationships. And while you might think that the two had to sacrifice some revenue to make these changes, that's not the case. In fact, they have both increased their profitability by 25 percent in less than a year. And if that doesn't catch your attention, maybe this will: since cleaning up their sales business, they've had to hire a coach to help them determine what to do with all the extra time they've freed up, which is currently about fifteen hours a week. Not a bad problem to have, is it?

Like Brian and Tres, have you ever had more than enough time to run your sales business? I bet the 100 percent question from the previous chapter was appealing to you because we'd all like to spend the majority of our workdays doing the few selling tasks we enjoy most. But since reading the question, perhaps you've asked, "Is it really possible?" If you did, you weren't the first person. The truth is, most salespeople probably have a hard time believing it's possible in the sales profession to spend the majority of their time doing the one or two things that they both enjoy and at which they excel. But it is possible, and it's not as difficult as you might think. In fact, it all starts by following the Law of the Broom.

IF YOU AREN'T PROACTIVE, YOU'RE REACTIVE

I recognize that there are probably thousands of different kinds of companies and products represented by the readers of this book. But regardless of the size or structure of your company, or the type of product you sell, there is one thing that is certain if you're involved in sales in any way: You could spend more time doing the things that advance your career if you could get rid of the things that are holding you back.

You could spend more time doing the things that advance your career if you could get rid of the things that are holding you back.

Now, that may seem rudimentary. But consider for a moment the following dilemmas that arise from a "messy" business:

➢ If you can't find the time to do things right, when will you find the time to do things over?

➢ If you spend most of your time with clients who don't completely trust you, where will you find time to build high trust with the right clients?

➢ If you don't have time to call your clients back, how will you make time to talk when they call you?

➢ If you don't have time to make quality sales, does your quantity of sales really matter?

Now consider the following reactionary truths:

> ➤ If you don't show customers your trustworthy way of doing business, they will assume you do business any way.

> ➤ If you hurry your sales, you usually end up waiting on sales.

> ➤ If you don't return calls, the calls return to you.

> ➤ If you don't have an assistant, you are your assistant.

> ➤ If you don't tell people when to call you, they will call you whenever they want.

> ➤ If you don't take advantage of your time, your time will take advantage of you.

Most of us understand the essence of reactionary relationships because of something we probably learned in high school science or physics class called Newton's Third Law of Motion, which says that for every action there is an equal and opposite reaction. The same phenomenon occurs in your sales business. One positive action usually elicits another positive action. One negative action, or no action at all, elicits another negative action. And generally speaking, there is only one remedy for avoiding the negative results of doing business in a reactive way; that's becoming proactive about how you do business.

When it comes to being reactive or proactive in your sales business, one trend tends to either solve or create the need for the other. In short, if you have not established clean systems and tight procedures to run your business effectively, then your business is being run by the people and activities of your days. Your sales business is reactive (not run by you) rather than proactive (run by you). And remember that high trust does not happen arbitrarily—it must be proactively earned.

On the other hand, when you take the time to clean up your business by establishing systems and procedures to effectively deal with the most common and most productive activities of your day, your business becomes proactive and is able to continually expand. More than that, when your business is cleaned up, your time is freed up to do what you do best and let others handle the rest. That's the essence of following the Law of the Broom.

GREEN-LIGHTING YOUR SALES BUSINESS

When you were fifteen years old, you probably spent many hours daydreaming about the prospects of driving that first car. You were knocking on the door of a new kind of freedom and independence, and you couldn't wait to get behind the wheel without Mom or Dad sitting next to you. Ready or not, you wanted that feeling of being in control of your own destiny each day—even if that only meant driving to school. Back then, driving symbolized independence—it gave you the ability to go when and where you wanted to go. Or at least that was the plan.

As your sixteenth birthday approached, you no doubt sat through driver's education classes and learned some pretty basic stuff designed not only to help you drive correctly, but also to save your life. While you most certainly knew what each of the colors of a traffic light already symbolized, a review was part of the class procedure because the colors on a traffic light are standard knowledge for driving effectively. And a few months later when you took your driving test, you probably made sure to pay close attention to the traffic lights on the road. You stopped when you came to a red light. You gave the car a little gas when the light turned green, making sure to not go too fast. And, as ridiculous as it may seem now, you probably even slowed down for a yellow light instead of speeding up.

But when you got your license, it was a different story. You just wanted to go. Didn't matter when or where. You just wanted to drive—the faster the better. Red lights suddenly became nuisances. Yellow lights became lighter shades of green. And green lights became icons of your newfound freedom. But, eventually you probably learned that there's more to driving a car when you received your first ticket or were involved in your first accident. There are laws for a reason, you learned. Laws that can be broken, yes. But laws carry penalties if broken. Penalties that can even take away your freedom.

I bet when you first started your sales career, something very similar happened. You learned the rules well enough to be given a license to sell something. And I bet you were even careful to do things by the book when you started, because you probably had someone watching your every move. But once you were given the keys to your selling independence, you just hit the gas pedal. Speed became the key to your success and freedom—selling to anyone and everyone as often as you could. Slowing down was out of the question—you had money to make. Therefore you considered anything that required you to slow your pace to be a hindrance to success.

That's how most new sales professionals are taught to sell, isn't it? Full speed ahead—never mind the signs. Quantity matters most—never mind quality. The problem is, you'll never be highly successful in the sales profession that way. That's because there are standards in the selling profession that regulate the speed at which you can sell effectively. Traffic lights of selling, so to speak, that indicate when you should go, when you should stop, and when you should slow down if your goal is to earn loyal, lucrative clients. Sure, you can always ignore the traffic lights, and even get away with it for a while. But eventually you'll get caught, and the results could be very destructive to your business.

Imagine what would happen to your sales business if you started to heed the traffic signals that lead to success. What would happen if your green-light activities—those that build high trust and earn you more money—increased? What would happen if you began to remove red-light activities—those that don't build high trust or increase your profits—by strategically heeding yellow lights long enough to determine then hone your most productive activities? The fact is, your days *should* be ordered this way.

Red-light activities include things such as

> ➤ filling out and filing paperwork

> ➤ faxing and copying

> ➤ managing crises

➢ dealing with high-maintenance/low-profit customers

➢ coping with telephone interruptions

➢ answering E-mail interruptions

➢ taking long lunches that aren't necessary

➢ hanging out with whiners instead of winners

➢ gossiping with coworkers

➢ randomly calling on prospects, or calling on "easy" prospects or clients who don't provide good business

These types of activities should be removed from your workload as much as possible so that the majority of your time is spent on green-light activities such as

➢ high trust relationship management and growth

➢ high trust partnership planning

➢ high trust referral follow-up

➢ new client prospecting

➢ high trust selling and reselling

➢ adding value to key clients

➢ adding value to key partners

And once you've removed red-light activities from your day, you can run your business as efficiently as possible, slowing down only at strategic times to determine if anything can be done better.

The 100 percent question asks you to consider what your career would look like if you spent all of your work hours on the few things that produced the greatest return for your time—if your path each day was illuminated with green-light activities.

Following the Law of the Broom helps you become more clear on what you need to do, and stop doing, to make the 100 percent question a reality—to green-light your sales business once and for all. And for most that begins when you slow down instead of speeding up.

SLOWING DOWN AND CLEANING UP

To be successful at high trust selling you must do more than seek out the green lights and avoid the red lights; you must also heed the yellow lights. As your sales business shifts to higher speeds, it will become necessary for you to streamline some of your practices and processes. The more high trust relationships you build, the more efficient your business needs to become.

When you're starting out (or restructuring the way you sell) you will spend extra time learning the trade of high trust selling; and that's necessary to build the foundation of your future success. But the more you master the tasks involved in high trust selling the less time-consuming they will be, and therefore the more profitable they will become. In essence, once you've removed from your day the activities that do not add value, the process of building an efficient high trust sales business is simply a matter of progressing toward a green-lit pathway.

Of course, to remain successful you will still need to observe yellow-light periods in order to ensure maximum efficiency; but when you're running your sales business efficiently, those periods of time will simply be a matter of strategy, not major restructuring. Some typical yellow-light activities successful salespeople invest time in developing are:

➤ improving product knowledge

➤ identifying the right new prospects

➤ generating and managing leads

➤ improving presentation skills

➤ improving objection-management skills

> creating marketing and advertising material

> creating follow-up material

These are the types of things in which it will take some time to reach maximum efficiency, especially if you have just inserted them into your daily or weekly routine. But whether your sales business is stopped, moving slowly, or a constant stop and go, now is your chance to clean things up.

It's usually not long after a major upshift in sales that a slow-down period becomes necessary. However, many successful salespeople make the mistake of blowing through the yellow lights and, as a result, end up having to stop and backtrack. This hurts their relationships as well as their profits.

Or it might be that you need to slow down right now, and it's not a result of tremendous sales growth. To the contrary, heeding a yellow light may be necessary because you've been trying to upshift your sales business without first cleaning up the processes that run it. That's like entering the Indy 500 with a Model-T Ford. If that's your situation, you've probably suffered your share of confusion, panic, and frustration. But if you're careful to heed the yellow lights now and down the road, regardless of your level of success, it's possible to avoid the red lights altogether.

Heeding a yellow light in your sales career is the equivalent of slowing down long enough to evaluate how you're using your time. If you're just starting out, that probably means slowing down for a brief period of time each day until you are comfortable with your sales practices, procedures, and performance. If you're further down the road, that may mean settling into something I call the "third Friday" routine, in which every third Friday of the month is reserved for slowing down enough to evaluate your selling efficiency. But whether it's daily, weekly, or a Friday per month, slowing down, making observations, and if necessary, charting a more profitable course of action is a hallmark trait of all top-producing, trustworthy salespeople—and it's the key to following the Law of the Broom.

Successful salespeople understand that producing greater profits means giving more and more of their time and energy to green-light activities. By increasing the time you spend on green-light activities and reducing the time you spend on red-light activities, you know they will eventually maximize the value of your time. But to do so you must slow down enough *now* to evaluate what is—and what is not—helping your progress, then commit to slowing down *later* at strategic times regularly as you continually grow your sales business.

THE BUILDING BLOCKS OF A HIGH TRUST BUSINESS

I ask people at almost every seminar this question: "How many of you have ever had a game plan for your day and by about 9:30 A.M it was thoroughly messed up?" Inevitably, I hear the chuckles and laughter. "Yep, that sounds like me," they say collectively. Then I ask, "How many of you stay relatively messed up the remainder of the day?" Again, almost everyone's hands shoot up. I then become very serious and ask, "How do you feel at the end of a day like that?" In more words or fewer, the collective answer is always, "We feel like the day was a waste." At one time, if Tom Ramirez had been in the audience when I asked those questions, his hand would have been raised high in the air.

Tom was a hard worker—maybe the hardest worker in his industry. And he had the numbers to show for it. He closed an average of one hundred orders a month and was making top dollar for his efforts. But there was a mounting problem. Although Tom was working very hard, he was not working very smart. In fact, to maintain the same level of business month after month, he was putting in eighty-hour workweeks. As Tom saw it, the long hours just came with the territory as a top sales producer. But as he would learn, it was a breakneck pace that could only last so long.

In 1992, Tom found himself in the ICU of a hospital near his home. He had suffered a brain aneurysm and would have to have surgery. It was time away from the job that Tom thought he couldn't afford—especially if he was going to maintain his productivity level. So as he sat on his hospital bed awaiting surgery, he began to make and field calls from three different phones, trying to overcome the inconvenient circumstances and meet his clients' needs as best he could. But before long the nurse came in and instructed him to stop working. She reminded him of the serious nature of his condition and that resting was absolutely critical. Tom reluctantly complied. But the nurse's words echoed in his head. In fact, for the first time in some time, Tom realized how destructive his long hours had become, not just to him but also to his young family. He realized that what really mattered was not how much money he made or how many sales he closed or even that every single client's need was met right away. What was most important was being alive to grow old with his wife, to see his two-year-old son become a man, and to see his two-month-old daughter grow into a beautiful woman.

When Tom came out of surgery and was readmitted to the ICU, it was his family whom he thought about—spending more time with them. With his current workload he wasn't sure how he could free up more time, but he determined to hire assistants to help him carry the workload, and a coach to help him work smarter. It would be the best move he had ever made in his sales career.

Before long, Tom's assistants were becoming his business partners, capable of carrying out every aspect of a sale. His coach was no longer teaching him how to increase productivity but instead how to have more life. Tom would be the first to tell you that during this "housecleaning" he was nervous. He knew that as he trained his assistants to become partners and began to delegate many of his tasks to them, his business would experience a drop-off in revenue. And he was right—although it was much smaller than he originally thought.

Nonetheless, with the encouragement and affirmation of his coach, Tom continued to revamp the way he worked until he had whittled his weekly hours down to forty. Then he began to focus on only carrying out the tasks he was best at, the green-light activities—namely, meeting top clients' needs and fostering productive, high trust relationships. Eventually, the unexpected started to happen. Tom and his team began to close more deals and produce more revenue than ever. In fact, today Tom and his team of partners close two hundred orders a month and bring in an average of $300 million in sales per year. Tom will quickly tell you that he never thought that kind of production was possible from a forty-hour workweek. But now he's a firm believer in the Law of the Broom.

TIME BLOCKING

Let me be very candid: If you experience wasted days, it's almost certainly because you're not running a clean sales business. Wasted days happen when you don't have a plan, when you lack vision, and when you're not clear on how to establish trust with customers. When you don't know how to say no to interruptions, marginal deals, or high-maintenance customers. When you wake up early to handle the stuff that didn't get done yesterday, then try make your cold calls without warming up, then attend a sales meeting that doesn't teach you a thing, then handle problem orders, then return calls to customers who are not satisfied, then become a courier, copy repairman, and coffee maker in one.

If you experience wasted days, it's almost certainly because you're not running a clean sales business.

Wasted days are rarely days without activity. Like Tom Ramirez's days, your days can be very full—just not fully productive and maybe even destructive. In short, wasted days happen when you allow red-light activities to rule your day. But to be highly successful and run a highly trustworthy sales business, you must find a better way to structure your time. And that begins when you create, implement, and master a skill called *time blocking*.

Time blocking is:

➤ scheduling your priorities rather than prioritizing your schedule

➤ predefining your green activities that are necessary for your business to excel

➤ incorporating green "blocks" of time into a daily schedule that helps you maintain a sense of predictability and certainty

➤ an efficient way for your clients and your team to remain apprised of your activities without your having to return calls and E-mails

➤ initially challenging but ultimately cost-effective

Time blocking is *not*:

➤ trying to not waste time

➤ a rigid declaration

➤ yellow Post-It notes all over your desk

➤ a "To do" list

➤ a quick fix

On the following page is an example of what a time-blocking schedule might look like.

Time blocking is the foundation of business efficiency; and you must commit to mastering this principle if you desire to build a booming sales business. The fundamental rationale for time blocking is the knowledge that if green activities don't get scheduled, they usually get done feebly, fruitlessly, or not at all. Therefore, great advances can be made if a salesperson determines to begin scheduling specific blocks of

Time	MONDAY	TUESDAY	WEDNESDAY	THURSDAY	FRIDAY	SATURDAY	SUNDAY
5:00 AM	Devotional	Devotional	Devotional	Devotional	Devotional		
6:00 AM	Workout-Cardio	Workout-Resistance	Workout-Cardio	Workout-Resistance	Workout-Cardio		
7:00 AM	Shower-Breakfast	Shower-Breakfast	Shower-Breakfast	Shower-Breakfast	Shower-Breakfast		
7:30 AM	AM Checklist	AM Checklist	AM Checklist	AM Checklist	AM Checklist	Family Breakfast	Early Church & Sunday School
8:00 AM	Lead Calls	Lead Calls	Lead Calls	Lead Calls	Lead Calls		
8:30 AM	Lead Calls	Lead Calls	Client Meetings	Client Meetings	Client Meetings		
9:00 AM	Team Meeting Product Knowledge	Implementation On-Time	Client Meetings	Client Meetings	Client Meetings		
9:30 AM							
10:00 AM							
10:30 AM	Lead Calls & E-Mail	Lead Calls & E-Mail	Lead Calls & E-Mail	Lead Calls & E-Mail	Lead Calls & E-Mail		
11:00 AM							Family Lunch
11:30 AM	Lead Calls & E-Mail	Open Lunch	Office Lunch	Strategic Partner Lunch	Open Lunch		
12:00 PM	One-on-One lunch						
12:30 PM							
1:00 PM	Client Meetings	Client Meetings	Client Meetings	Client Meetings	Client Meetings		
1:30 PM							
2:00 PM							
2:30 PM							
3:00 PM	Lead Calls & E-Mail	Lead Calls & E-Mail	Lead Calls & E-Mail	Lead Calls & E-Mail	Lead Calls & E-Mail		
3:30 PM							
4:00 PM	Client Meetings	Client Meetings	Client Meetings	Client Meetings	Client Meetings		
4:30 PM							
5:00 PM	PM Checklist	PM Checklist	PM Checklist	PM Checklist	PM Checklist		
5:30 PM							
6:00 PM	Family Dinner Kids Bath & Kids Reading	Family Dinner Kids Bath & Kids Reading	Family Dinner Kids Bath & Kids Reading	Date Night	Family Dinner Kids Bath & Kids Reading	Family Dinner Kids Bath & Kids Reading	Family Dinner Kids Bath & Kids Reading
7:00 PM							
8:00 PM							
9:00 PM							
10:00 PM	Bed	Bed	Bed	Bed	Bed	Bed	Bed

Tues: Team Lunch out of office once per month 11:30-1
Tues: Team Celebration out of office once per month 4-6 PM

Alternate cardio and resistance workouts every week

1st Friday: Business Planning out of office
2nd Friday: Host Site Visits
3rd and 4th Friday: 8:00-Noon Implementation time
5th Friday: Write Book

time for green activities, and commits to not spending time on red activities until green activities are done.

If you've been running a messy business for a while, it may take a few months for you to sweep out all the red activities from your routine. But don't be discouraged. Just make it your goal to clean up the mess one red activity at a time until you reach the point at which you are spending the majority of your day on green, productive activities.

If you've never used time blocking in your sales business, a good way to begin is by committing the first hour of each workday to green activities. Make a sale, secure a prospect, set an appointment, manage a lead, add value to a current client, or prepare for future presentations; but don't handle urgencies, crises, or interruptions until your second hour. Then maintain this timetable: one hour for green activities, one hour for red activities—for the remainder of the day. If you follow this schedule faithfully from 8:00 A.M. until 5:00 P.M., taking a one-hour lunch along the way, you will have blocked four hours for green activities and four hours for red activities. That's a good foundation to start with. And here's the beauty in time blocking: If you were currently productive for only 25 percent of your day, you have just doubled your high trust selling time. Soon, your increase in productive time blocks will build a significantly larger profit base.

COMMENCING CONSTRUCTION

Starting with the next chapter, I will share with you several proven green-light strategies for boosting your selling success through the roof. In fact, as a result of the coming strategies you will be in a position to double, triple, and even quadruple your business in the next year if you are able to insert them effectively into your daily routine. And that's why time blocking is so important for you to implement now, before you begin taking on more clients. The Law of the Broom says that you must get your business running as efficiently as possible so that when the increase in sales come—and it will come—you will have the means to handle it with excellence and integrity. To do so you must see each strategy as a weapon to increase your arsenal of green activities. You must see each new strategy as another block that will add to the stability and longevity of your business. Do that throughout the rest of this book, and by the time we're through you'll have built a much bigger business than you've ever imagined.

SALES LEADERSHIP APPLICATION

As the leader of a sales team, how you use your time directly affects your ability to empower your people to make the most of theirs. Spend some time making sure your time-blocking schedule is accurate and consistent. This might require you to rethink some of the tasks that take from the time you can spend developing your people. If you don't currently have enough time to regularly invest in the sales success of your people, then you need to clean up your own schedule so that you do. Once you've determined what can be cleaned up to free up more time for your people, discipline yourself to stick with your new routine. Only then can you teach your people with integrity how to build their sales business on productive time blocks.

SECTION II

LAYING THE FOUNDATION FOR BUILDING
A TRUSTWORTHY SALES BUSINESS

The Law of the Dress Rehearsal

*Practicing Your Lines Elevates
the Level of Your Performance*

Y ou would probably be amazed at the amount of preparation that goes into a first-rate production. But that's true of every great performance—especially in sales. Remember earlier when I shared with you my first experience with Tom Hopkins? One thing I didn't tell you was that Tom's presentation that day covered six hours and included a thirty-five-page workbook for each participant. Pretty normal as far as seminars are concerned.

But there was something about that day that was very abnormal—in a surprising way. Early in the seminar, I noticed that Tom had not gone to the podium to look at his notes for almost thirty minutes, yet he walked us through the workbook without missing a single word. It made an impression on me, so I continued to make this observation as the day went on. A few times I found myself wondering if he had sneaked a peak at his notes while I was writing something down. Surely, I thought, he had to look at some point. Near the end of the seminar, as Tom was discussing the importance of scripting and mastering sales presentations, he noted, "If you observed me closely today, you noticed that I did not look at my teaching notes once. That's because I have spent over one hundred hours making sure I know my stuff so I can effectively and convincingly present the information to you."

I was impressed when he made it thirty minutes without notes. But the entire seminar? That was truly amazing, and it made a lasting impression on my young sales mind. I acknowledged that mastering my "lines" was something very important to my success as a sales professional.

And if you're serious about reaching the peak of your selling potential, you must acknowledge the same. You must *know* your lines. You must *know* your presentation. You must *know* the next step. In the process of selling, you don't have time to think about it. You don't have time to flip through the pages of your "How to Sell" manual if you're interested in earning a customer's trust. The truth is that if you want to be a world-class sales professional there are two things you should never have to think about:

1. how to sell

2. what to say in a selling situation

Remember the popular prime-time show hosted by Dick Clark and Ed McMahon called *TV's Bloopers and Practical Jokes*? For an hour we laughed as we watched some of the best actors thoroughly mess up their lines. We laughed because it's very human to make mistakes. And seeing actors make bloopers reminded us that despite the flawless performances we saw on their television shows even the very best actors forget their lines from time to time.

But have you ever made a blooper in sales? Ever said something you shouldn't have said or done something stupid then wished with everything in you that someone would just yell, "Cut!" so you could start again? I have—and it doesn't feel good. That's because in sales, unlike television, you don't get a second chance to retake your lines. You don't have a production crew to edit out your bloopers and create the impression of a flawless performance. In sales, once a word or an action is out, it's out, and you can never reel it back in. You can't undo the negative impression it may have created or regain the sale it may have lost. Sales is a live performance day in and day out—like a Broadway play, where most mistakes are noticed, and where one wrong move can jeopardize the entire performance if you're not careful.

Consider for a moment: What do the following have in common?

➤ *Riverdance*

➤ *Cirque du Soleil*

➤ An N'SYNC concert

➤ *The Phantom of the Opera*

➤ The President's State of the Union Address

The answer: Every performer involved in each top-notch production spends more time practicing the production than they ever do performing the production. And the same must be true of you, if you desire to build a successful, high trust business. You must practice more than you play so that when the curtain comes up you know what to say. That's the Law of the Dress Rehearsal.

A HIGH TRUST PERFORMANCE DOESN'T JUST HAPPEN

Unfortunately, the truth is that most salespeople are not prepared to succeed when opportunities present themselves. Most salespeople are not sure how to proceed in a selling situation, but they do anyway, right or wrong. They're not sure what to say in a selling situation, but they speak anyway, right or wrong. They usually end up talking too much and listening too little. And when the curtain comes down, they wonder why the customer didn't applaud with approval. Unfortunately, most salespeople are not prepared to earn a customer's trust, so they generally don't. That's why the average salesperson has to make dozens of sales attempts before landing one sale. That's because high trust doesn't just happen. While you can haphazardly persuade, manipulate, or con customers into buying your product or service from time to time, you can't earn their authentic trust and lasting business that way.

The Law of the Dress Rehearsal says that to give a great performance you must be well practiced. In other words, to be highly successful you must know what to say and do when a sales opportunity

117

arises. You must know how to earn high trust initially, then foster high trust permanently. That's what it means to follow the Law of the Dress Rehearsal.

THE HIGH TRUST SELLING SYSTEM (HTSS)

Over the next six chapters, I am going to lead you through one of the most profound and productive sales systems ever designed. The High Trust Selling System (HTSS) has been field tested by sales professionals of every shape and size for the last twenty-two years. My team and I also use the system and generate millions of dollars in sales every year. In fact, thousands of my company's clients have effectively implemented the system into their selling practice, and most have doubled, tripled, or quadrupled their sales and their paychecks in as little as one year. And I am certain the same can be true for you if you're willing to implement and adhere to the system in your business.

Before I explain the High Trust Selling System, think about some important questions that will help till the soil of your business mind and prepare it for the very fruitful seeds to come.

- ➤ Do you have trouble talking to prospects?
- ➤ Do you have a firmly imprinted process in your mind that leads any prospect from inaction to action and allows him or her to naturally and enthusiastically say "Yes" when you ask for an appointment or business?
- ➤ Do you have trouble using the phone to effectively set appointments?
- ➤ Do you have challenges maintaining control of appointments?
- ➤ When you make a call, are you thinking revenue (commissions) or relationship (mega commissions)?
- ➤ During the presentation phase of an appointment, do you know in advance what you are going to say, or do you tend to wing it?

➤ When you get an objection, do you know precisely how to respond?

➤ When someone says "No," do you know how to turn that prospect into a transition client who in the next thirty to 365 days will become a client for life?

➤ When someone says "Yes," do you have a retention system so you can continue to add value to him or her as the relationship grows?

➤ When someone asks you, "How much does it cost?" do you freeze up and fumble with your words?

➤ Are you confident in how you sell? If so, in what is your confidence?

If you're like most salespeople, you probably don't have a good answer for some of the previous questions, and that's OK—for now. The purpose of this chapter and the six chapters that follow is to give you the right answers. To give you confidence in your selling process so that you can gain the confidence and high trust of your clients, and in turn build a steadfast business. Hopefully, the first seven chapters taught you how to lay the foundation necessary to become a trust-worthy salesperson. From this point on we will discuss how to lay the foundation necessary for building a trustworthy sales business. Consider this chapter and specifically the High Trust Selling System as the bridge that will link your *salesperson* foundation with your *sales business* foundation.

The HTSS describes the four "Acts" that must be performed effectively if you desire to build a high trust sales business. In sales it's not enough to be a trustworthy person. While it's certain that you must have a trustworthy foundation within you (beneath the surface) to be highly successful, high trust selling is still about taking action; the right action. Therefore to become a trustworthy salesperson with a trustworthy sales business you must not only know *why* you are selling, you must also know *how* to sell during each act of the process.

You must know how to apply yourself, so to speak. That's why the Law of the Dress Rehearsal is so critical—because the better you know how to sell, the better you will perform. And every steadfast business is built one sales performance at a time.

Act 1: The Approach
The Right Prospecting Technique
to Land a High Trust Appointment

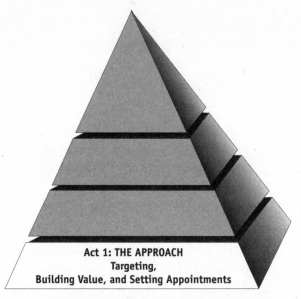

Act 1: THE APPROACH
Targeting,
Building Value, and Setting Appointments

THE HIGH TRUST SALES PYRAMID

Every high trust business is built on a foundation of prospecting; therefore every prospecting call must establish a foundation of value and trust if it is to successfully land an appointment. Ideally, prospecting begins before an attempt is made to secure an appointment with a potential prospect. As the one doing the selling, it makes sense to pre-qualify the individual that is highly likely to have a need for your product or service. Once an individual has been established as a solid prospect, the approach can then be made with confidence. The problem is that very few salespeople actually enjoy this part of the selling process because they aren't confident in the process with which they go about it.

Most mediocre salespeople sit around waiting for the phone to ring. They hope someone will call them, and magically, that person will be a perfect fit for their product or service. Occasionally such salespeople will send out a bag of letters (because the rejection of a letter is much easier to deal with), but they never follow up on them. Or they get leads from their company but after ten rejections they can't get very excited about making the eleventh call. Then they blame the product or the company's poor marketing and advertising for their poor performance. The truth, however, is that mediocre salespeople never take full responsibility for their own actions. And selling is the salesperson's show, the salesperson's performance. Therefore you must own your lines if you are to ever excel.

Selling is the salesperson's show, the salesperson's performance. Therefore you must own your lines if you are to ever excel.

High trust salespeople open their show with an entirely different technique than most, and that technique is the key to their superb prospecting performance. The foundation for successful selling starts with a compelling opening act, which I call "The Approach." The Approach refers to both prospecting and appointment setting. This is where call reluctance (or stage fright) usually rears its ugly head. But the number-one reason why salespeople experience stage fright in the opening Act is because their approaches, historically, have not conveyed high value or created high trust. But successful salespeople have rehearsed their lines and believe that what they bring to the stage is highly valuable and highly trustworthy. As a result, they experience less reluctance and more excitement.

The key to a compelling approach is to become passionate about your purpose and product and the value they can add to your prospect. A passionate salesperson can make the buying process fun. In fact, you should never make a prospecting call without a purpose. You see, your prospecting audience will only be receptive to you if what you have to offer is compelling to them. Imagine what you would do if you sat down to a show that was billed as a blockbuster performance, but after the first few lines it felt more like a flop, or worse, was an entirely different show altogether, one that you had no interest in seeing. That's what it's like when you try to call on a random prospect without having prepared your lines. But when you're well rehearsed and confident in your opening lines, and when you take the time to call on the right prospect, you will experience far more approval than rejection.

Act 2: The Interview
Creating High Trust with a Prospect

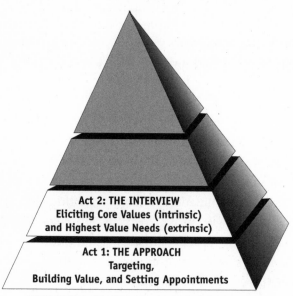

Act 2: THE INTERVIEW
Eliciting Core Values (intrinsic)
and Highest Value Needs (extrinsic)

Act 1: THE APPROACH
Targeting,
Building Value, and Setting Appointments

THE HIGH TRUST SALES PYRAMID

Once you have the attention of a qualified prospect, the second thing you must rehearse and master is how to effectively conduct a High Trust Client Interview. An effective interview is a discipline that all top-performing sales people have mastered. If you don't master the

High Trust Client Interview, your sales career will flounder, you will lose money, and you will usually end up working with prospects that will bring you grief.

When teaching the High Trust Client Interview in my seminars, I break the audience into groups of two. I have each group determine who is going to go first and then tell them that when I say "Go," the first interviewer has thirty seconds to sell his or her pen to the other person. As I listen to their interviewing techniques, I find most of them are doing the one thing they shouldn't—they are talking. I yell, "Stop," and as they have all been trained, they keep on selling, keep on talking, keep on trying to close. I appreciate their tenacity. However, high trust salespeople know that initially there is an inverse relationship between talking and getting the sale.

To follow up on this exercise, I ask the audience this question: "Before you started telling the prospect everything your pen could do for him or her, how many of you asked, 'What's important about owning a pen to you?'" Rarely do any hands go up. I continue, "How many of you were 100 percent certain that the pen you were selling was the one your prospect would want?" Again, few, if any, hands go up. I press on, "How many of you were certain your prospect was in the market for a pen before you started selling it?" No hands. The case is built—the audience understands, as must you, that a vital part of selling is asking the right questions so that what you sell and what a client wants match up. If you skip this Act, you will experience resistance, which comes in the form of stalls, objections, or noes. And what's worse, you might remove any opportunity for future business. The result of a poor performance in Act 2 is having to make more calls on more people to get the numbers you want; and that probably doesn't give you the life you want because it means more hours on the job and less time off.

To perform well in Act 2 you must learn that the key to selling is not selling; it is providing. And the key to providing is knowing in advance what to provide. Neither can be accomplished without mastering the art of asking value-adding questions, then listening to what your prospects tell you. And so you don't misunderstand, the mind-set of a top performer is void of manipulation or shady tactics. Top-notch performers are always thinking win-win.

> **You must learn that the key to selling is not selling;
> it is providing. And the key to providing is
> knowing in advance what to provide.**

Our research indicates that there are valuable benefits in mastering the ability to listen before you sell. It shows that the more questions you ask, the more needs you discover. And discovering values and needs is the very purpose of the High Trust Client Interview.

KEY QUESTIONS TO GET YOU THINKING

In the example I gave from my seminar, it would be important for sales professionals who are in the writing instrument business to ask these questions in advance of selling a pen:

> ➢ What's important to the prospect about owning a pen?

> ➢ What type of pen design does the prospect typically favor?

> ➢ What type of ink cartridge does the prospect desire?

> ➢ What color of ink is the prospect's favorite?

> ➢ What is the prospect's budget for the next pen he or she buys?

> ➢ How many pens does the prospect buy in one year?

The answers to such questions are critical because without them you will have to ad-lib your sales presentation. Put it this way, without the knowledge gained from the questions above, you could not *know* the emotional motivation for the prospect's pen purchase, nor could you know the logical factors that make up his buying strategy. Cap or push-button? Rolling ball, ballpoint, or old-fashioned ink tips?

Black or blue ink? A BiC or a Mont Blanc budget? His average repurchase rate? On the other hand, if you knew such details up front there's no doubt you'd have a much easier time selling pens or whatever it is you sell.

Once you have successfully interviewed your prospect, the third Act in your selling performance is presenting solutions to your prospect's needs. While on rare occasion you may be able to ad-lib your way through the first two Acts, in Act 3 you must be well prepared. This is the point at which preparation must meet with opportunity if you're going to be successful.

Act 3: The Solution
Offering Trustworthy Solutions to Your Prospect's Needs

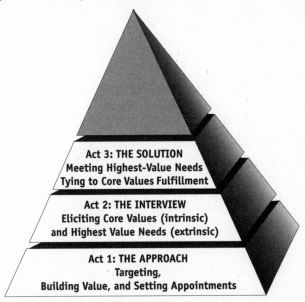

THE HIGH TRUST SALES PYRAMID

All high trust salespeople are in a constant pursuit to discover needs for which they can offer solutions. You must be in the solution business to give a successful performance in Act 3. I learned this early on in my career and the result was nothing short of huge—my income went up 300 percent in less than one year. In fact, the key was something one of my early mentors told me: that there are basically ten reasons why a prospect would use you and ten reasons why they would use your company. He said that all I had to do was learn those twenty things, develop scripts to effectively address them, and then memorize those scripts. So that's what I did. For four weeks I interviewed my customers to learn their needs. I then scripted my solutions to their specific needs so I would never lose a sale again from lack of preparation. You need to do the same thing. I will cover this in greater detail in a coming chapter, but for now, get to thinking about the needs of your prospects.

Below are some of the needs that I hear expressed in the marketplace on a consistent basis. See if they are similar to your existing clients' reasons for working with you.

You:

- Experience
- Knowledge
- Integrity
- Professionalism
- Communication
- Accessibility
- Flexibility
- Responsiveness

Your Company:

- Location
- Delivery
- Product/Technical support
- Reputation

- ➤ Innovativeness
- ➤ Financial Strength
- ➤ Market Share
- ➤ Product Line
- ➤ Research and Development

Whatever the needs may be, you must have answers, and you must be confident in how you present them. That is the key to a solid performance in Act 3.

Act 4: The Action
Asking for the Prospect's Business

THE HIGH TRUST SALES PYRAMID

Once you have offered effective solutions to your prospect, the fourth and final Act in a high trust selling presentation is asking for the business. I find that this area of the selling process is where my views differ most from other sales authors and trainers. Many sales success manuals and books teach you to ask for a prospect's business constantly. They tell you it takes several attempts to finally gain a sale—but that is only true if you haven't performed well in the first three Acts. The key to your performance in Act 4 is to understand that people will want to do business with you if and only if they trust you. In other words, if a prospect doesn't trust you, she won't buy from you, no matter what you do or how many times you ask for the business. But even if she does trust you, you will not ascertain her business if you don't ask for it. The key is to ask for business only when you have

➤ thoroughly understood the prospect's needs and buying strategy,

➤ completely answered the prospect's needs and questions with your solutions, and

➤ confirmed an indication that the prospect would like to proceed.

When you're careful to ask for a prospect's business at the right time, you won't continue to hear the wrong answer.

INTERMISSION: OBJECTION MANAGEMENT DEEPENING A CUSTOMER'S LEVEL OF TRUST

By the time we're to the end of this book, you will see why most high trust salespeople rarely have to deal with objections. But objection management is a valuable skill if you desire to be a top sales performer. And it's important to note that objections can occur during any part of your presentation. The fact that we are discussing this last is not an indication that all objections occur after you ask for business—though that is where they most often occur. Just think of objection management as an intermission in your sales performance that can happen at any time, but ideally not at all.

There are only two reasons you will ever get an objection. First, if you have not thoroughly and convincingly solved the prospect's stated needs. This is either because you don't know them or your solutions were weak. In other words, you have not yet created enough value or trust. Second, if your prospect fears the change that a commitment may bring. But regardless of the reason for the objection, the key to objection management is to not lose with sloppy management the rapport you have built.

Objections are not obstacles—they are opportunities to further a relationship and advance a sale.

Objections are not obstacles—they are opportunities to further a relationship and advance a sale. You need to think this way. Objections are not insurmountable if you're prepared. What I don't like about most sales success manuals is that they teach you to "overcome" an objection. But I'm here to tell you that if you try to overcome objections, you will lose more sales than you win. Instead, the key is to become successful at *managing* objections by preparing beforehand how you will respond. And the good news is that there are not very many objections. They don't change much over the years. Preparing for them is simply a matter of learning what they are and then rehearsing your responses.

I get excited when I receive objections because it usually tells me that the prospect is still interested in our dialogue. But what I want you to understand is that objections are not necessarily signs that your performance is flat. Some prospects will object just because they can. Your job is simply to be prepared for them when they do. But the fact is that if you are committed to mastering the High Trust Selling System, you will become such a top-notch performer that you will rarely have to deal with objections at all.

Jim McMahan is the one sales professional I know who best personifies what we're talking about. When he began his sales career in 1986, Jim was very motivated to succeed. He was twenty-six years old, jobless, living on his wife's salary, with a child on the way. He didn't have time to dawdle, so he immediately began to study successful salespeople, trying as best he could to comprehend and model their strategies and techniques. That's when Jim was first introduced to the Law of the Dress Rehearsal. He bought into the idea of preparing responses and set out to observe twenty of the most critical sales situations in order to gain the proper knowledge for creating powerful scripts that would prepare him to excel in key sales situations. And excel he did. In fact, with his scripted responses in place and some rehearsal under his belt, Jim's effectiveness and credibility increased dramatically.

In one instance, Jim's coworker asked him to help give a sales presentation to a potential client. He was glad to help out even though he stood to gain no business from the meeting. Or so he thought. Jim sat down in the meeting with his coworker and his coworker's prospect and gave a confident presentation just as he'd rehearsed. He answered questions eloquently and put to rest all of the prospect's objections and hang-ups. And in the end what happened was unexpected. He won the prospect's confidence. She was so impressed with his presentation savvy and objection management that she recruited him to do business with her. And that was more than just a flattering pat on the back for Jim. Today, the two still foster a strategic partnership from which Jim earns over seven figures a year. That's what can happen when you follow the Law of the Dress Rehearsal.

But we've only discussed the outline for a successful sales presentation. Let's get down to the details within each Act that are necessary to build a high trust business. That begins with the Law of the Bull's-Eye.

SALES LEADERSHIP APPLICATION

As the leader of a sales team, one of your main jobs is to help your people prepare for their sales presentations. To do so in the most effective manner, it may be necessary for you to become more involved in the selling process that your people carry out. In many cases, sales managers and team leaders are not personally involved in day-to-day selling. But I suggest that if you desire to add the most value to your people's presentations you make a point to do some selling of your own on a monthly basis to not only understand what customers your people are interacting with, but also to make sure that your presentation skills are honed enough to teach others effectively. In short, by spending one day a month (or whatever you feel is necessary) selling your company's products and/or services, you will ensure that you are never out of touch with the audience to which your team's presentations are made.

The Law of the Bull's-Eye

*If You Don't Aim for the Best Prospects,
You're Likely to Do Business with Any Prospect*

I'm fascinated by the sport of archery, especially the acute accuracy that's required to excel. Have you ever studied the moves of an archer? Have you ever watched him take an arrow, place it on the bow, draw the string back ever so slowly, pause to aim, and then release? Maybe you caught some of the archery events in the Winter Olympics. If you did then you know that the best archers follow the same routine every time, so much so that shooting an arrow at the bull's-eye is like second nature. In fact, if you watched a professional archer shoot an arrow again and again, you'd know that being a great archer has nothing to do with luck—especially after you witnessed four out of five shots sink into the center of the target. Plain and simple, the best archers know what it takes to hit the bull's-eye. And if you're going to master high trust selling, so must you.

The Law of the Bull's-Eye says that if you don't aim for the best prospects you will do business with any prospect. That's because in sales, as in archery, if you aren't aiming for the bull's-eye, you won't beat your competition very often. On the other hand, when you're good at hitting the bull's-eye prospects in your field, you can upstage your competition on a regular basis.

In Linda Davidson's case, bull's-eye prospecting will lead to the sale of three hundred more units this year alone, totaling $30 to 40 million in additional sales revenue. And that's no accident. You see, Linda is very purposeful about prospecting. She only shoots for the best—and when she hits them, she knows how to meet their needs better than the competition. As a result, her prospects become her clients for good.

For Linda, sometimes the reward of precise prospecting comes quickly. Other times it takes a longer investment. But because her aim is accurate, her prospecting almost always leads to major profits.

For example, Linda established a trustworthy relationship with a prospect that didn't come to fruition until four years later. Why did she continue fostering the relationship so long? She knew the particular prospect—who was loyal to one of her competitors—was one of the best clients in her industry. In other words, the potential return was well worth the investment. And as it turned out, she was right on. When her competitor failed to come through on a big deal, the prospect immediately called her. Linda set up a meeting in which she and the prospect came to terms with not only the deal on the table but also many deals in the future—the client transferred loyalty. That client now accounts for approximately $750,000 a month in sales for Linda. That's hitting the bull's-eye, something Linda continues to do on a regular basis.

In fact, to give you an idea of how good Linda is at hitting the bull's-eye, consider this: On January 1 of one year, she compiled a "wish list" of the nineteen top prospects in her field. By just over halfway through the year, Linda was already doing business with ten of the prospects on her list. And of the nine that remained, she had found three of the prospects to be unworthy of her investment, leaving just six to pursue. Only the best remain on Linda's prospecting list. But even those that are worthy of her investment don't remain on the list long—it's just a matter of time before they become Linda's clients for life.

THE PRACTICAL PSYCHOLOGY OF PROFITABLE PROSPECTING

The fact is that even if you have great interviewing skills, great presentation skills, and great objection management skills, but don't have the right prospects, none of that really matters. Obviously, nothing is sold without someone to sell it to. Therefore, if you're not prospecting, your business is dying. Prospecting is the blood that will keep your sales business alive. And not just when you're starting off. Prospecting is not an on-and-off switch; it is a volume dial that is turned up when you want more business and turned down when business is cruising. But there is a right and wrong way to gaining prospects, and you must understand the difference.

> **It doesn't matter how many prospects you see.**
> **It matters how you see the right prospects.**

To a certain extent, all of us play the numbers game in selling. However, it is erroneous to assume that if you see more people you will get more business. It's true that you usually need more prospects when you are starting your sales career than when you're established. But in either case, it's not the numbers that ultimately count. It doesn't matter how many prospects you see. It matters how you see the right prospects.

Would you rather see ten prospects and get one sale, or see one prospect and get one sale? Easy answer, right? It never feels good to have nine prospects say no. Your confidence and profits are only impacted positively by how many people say yes, not by how many calls you make. Therefore, prospecting is a productivity game, not a numbers game. And to maximize your prospecting efficiency you must replace the traditional "more is better" quantity concept with a "less is best" quality concept as you master the Law of the Bull's-Eye in your career. This is especially critical when you consider how much time prospecting can take from your day if it doesn't produce sales.

Profitable, efficient prospecting requires that you understand that your prospects will become clients who are either time abusers or time users. They can be categorized in one of the following four profiles:

1. **Low profit/high maintenance:** Prospects that have potential to produce a little business and a few referrals and are very hard to serve because of unrealistic price and service demands and inefficient business practices

2. **High profit/high maintenance:** Prospects that have potential to produce a lot of business and some referrals but are very hard to service because of unrealistic price and service demands, inefficient business practices, and a high need for ego fulfillment

3. **Low profit/low maintenance:** Prospects that have potential to produce a little business and a few referrals but are likely to provide greater profits as the relationship grows, and are easy to serve because of a high level of professionalism, strong desire to partner with you, and efficient business practices

4. **High profit/low maintenance:** Prospects that have potential to produce a lot of business and many referrals and are easy to serve because of a high level of professionalism, strong desire to partner with you, and efficient business practices

Prospect types 3 and 4 are obviously the kinds of people you want to work with on a regular basis. Type 2 prospects could be good to aim for, but only if you could lower the level of time and energy it takes to serve them. However, my experience is that the process of trying to convert a type 2 to a type 4 prospect usually takes more time than it's worth, especially when there are many more qualified prospects available. Type 1 prospects are generally never going to be worth doing business with. In short, type 1 and 2 prospects like to say no or grind you on price and service, and they are unreasonably untrusting. Type 3 and 4 prospects like to say yes and with high trust established will usually prove to be great clients.

Whether you sell sophisticated computer solutions or more simplistic imaging equipment, homes or loan services, Mercedes or Fords, business opportunities or office supplies, financial planning, legal advice, or accounting services—all sales presentation success is predicated on hitting the right prospects who will in turn become clients that reap high returns for life.

> **All sales presentation success is predicated on hitting the right prospects who will in turn become clients that reap high returns for life.**

I am constantly amazed at how many sales are left on the table when salespeople fail to think long-term. But if you prospect with the purpose of landing the right clients for life, you will resolve to be purposeful in securing their initial trust. What you do between the time you meet a person and the time that individual decides to buy determines whether he or she will become your client or your competition's. Here are some examples from my own experience:

➤ A car salesman asks for my card and calls me once, three weeks later. By that time I had already bought a car from another dealership that communicated with me six times before I picked the car up and five times after I drove it off the lot. The result was that the first salesperson lost a $50,000 sale; the second gained my trust.

➤ Sixty-five real estate agents get my name but only one follows up, and poorly. I buy from none of them. I call a sixty-sixth agent and after three meetings, I select him and use his services three times in five years, totaling $65,000 in commissions for the salesperson.

➤ As a salesperson, one particular client didn't give me her first order until eighteen months after she knew she was my prospect. During that time I communicated with her eighty-one times, trying to add value each time, so that I would ultimately be selected as her vendor. In the end, she became my best and most profitable client.

What I want you to understand to this point is that aiming for the best prospects is not cold-calling everyone and their mothers. It's not randomly phoning someone whose name you've never seen before that moment. It's not walking into an office that you've never been to and trying to meet with someone with whom you've never communicated. It's not leaving a business card on a restaurant table, under a windshield wiper, or on someone's front door. High trust selling has nothing to do with the luck of the draw or the alignment of the stars. Prospecting that leads to high trust sales and long-term clients has everything to do with preparation (knowing how to take accurate aim) and execution (knowing when to release).

> **High trust selling has nothing to do with the luck of the draw or the alignment of the stars.**

SELLING STARTS EARLY

I bet if you sat down and watched the movies that were taken of you when you were a child, you'd probably notice that your selling career began very early in life. In fact, you were probably trying to influence others from the word *go*. The bottom line back then was that if you wanted something badly, you figured out what needed to be done to get it.

Perhaps you recall your first selling effort. Think back. It may have been selling candy to raise money for Little League or cookies for the Girl Scouts or raffle tickets for school, but there was probably a point in your life when your "informal" sales career began. My first real recollection of selling was when I was in Little League at the age of eight.

I remember my dad telling me that if I wanted to sell the candy, I had to go to where the people were. He also assured me that it was highly unlikely that the doorbell would start ringing if I just sat at home and watched cartoons. I didn't know it then but that was my first introduction to the importance of prospecting the right people versus selling to any person. Taking my dad's advice, I did what every budding salesperson would do—I made a list of everyone I knew who would buy candy from me, highlighting those whom I thought would buy the most. After making my list, I figured out what I was going to say and hit my neighborhood streets. Within two days, I was sold out, when everyone else had barely begun. It's too bad I didn't remember my young sales experience when I began my first real sales job.

To my recollection, I didn't have substantial preparation before my first real day in the field where I actually had to sell something to make a living. And by then, my dad was no longer in the next room to tell me how to do it. My professional sales preparation was more like, "Here's your desk. Here's your phone. Good luck, Todd—you're on your own." Maybe that's why my first day in the field as a professional salesperson was so memorable for the wrong reasons.

The bottom line was that I made no sales—after over a hundred calls. And since that was not a feeling I was interested in revisiting, I immediately stopped selling that way and instead asked myself why that had happened. The answer came at 4:00 P.M. as I watched one of my competitors make a call. He came through the front door with a look of confidence. He beamed with excitement. He professionally announced himself to the receptionist then was ushered to the office of the prospect on which he was calling. About forty-five minutes later he came out of the office shaking hands with his new client and said, "I look forward to a long and profitable partnership with you." He had done something that had eluded me all day long. He had secured a new client. After seeing this, I thought, *How could I have that, and how soon?* The answer, I learned, was that I could have it as soon as I wanted. And the same is true for you.

Here's what I learned in the next several days as I began to purposefully observe other successful salespeople like the one on my first day. First, it seemed they made fewer calls than most, but had a much higher conversion rate to sales. And it seemed that the prospects they called on were more motivated to meet with them than to resist. Furthermore, it seemed that their appointments generally took a little longer than most but produced more positive results. And finally, it seemed by all accounts that they were making a lot more money than anyone else. Those observations inspired me greatly, so I started modeling them—and my business took off.

Like the successful salespeople whom I studied, I just did a few things different to elevate my success.

1. I always tried to determine another client or vendor who knew my prospects' names so I could use them in my introduction. This helped build credibility and trust and reduce tension.

2. I never "cold-called" again but made my cold calls warm, my warm calls hot, and my hot calls sizzle by sending a letter in advance of calling for an appointment.

3. I always made sure my initial letters had a Unique Value Proposition—something embedded in the letter that would genuinely pique their attention and captivate their interest.

4. I kept every phone call in which I asked for a business development appointment to less than ninety seconds whether I called the prospects or they called me. I committed to discovering needs and offering solutions in person rather than on the phone.

5. I sent a thank-you letter and a testimonial from an existing client to my prospects two days before meeting with them.

As a result of this change in approach, my sales began to soar and I became one of the top salespeople in my company in a matter of months. I want to help you do the same. In the remainder of this chapter I will show you how following the Law of the Bull's-eye can help you hit the best prospects in your sales business. Like an Olympic archer, it will help you fashion a prospecting routine that

. ensures you hit the bull's-eye prospects in your targeted field nearly every time you shoot.

GET READY . . .

I think that it is absolutely critical that you prepare for prospecting well, but please know that there is a point when you have to act. If all you do is take aim, you will never hit the bull's-eye, and worse, you will rarely get any business.

Due to past experiences with an inadequate form of prospecting you may be a little bow-shy at first, and I understand that. But for the remainder of this chapter let me help you gain some confidence by teaching you how to get ready, aim, and fire at prospects who are most likely to take your business to the next level.

Step #1: Secure your business plan. To achieve sales goals you must first set your prospecting goals. You may have already established these after reading Chapter 4, but let's review those steps here, applying them to prospecting.

Securing your business plan requires that you take the following steps.

1) Establish your volume goals. If you desire a six-figure income, your first year might look something like this:

   Income goal: $100,000
   Sales needed: 100 (if $1000 avg. earnings per sale)

2) Determine your daily numbers. Following our example above, it would look like this:

   If 100 sales are needed over the course of 250 workdays per year, you will need to close 2 sales every week or 1 sale every 2.5 days.

   100 sales / 250 working days = 1 sale every 2.5 working days

3) Determine your conversion goal. This refers to the percentage of sales you want to make per sales attempts. Following the example, it would look like this:

If your goal is to close 1 sale for every 2 sales attempts you make, your conversion rate goal would be 50%.

100 sales per year @ 50% conversion rate = 200 sales attempts needed

Then, by simply increasing the percentage of prospects that you turn to sales can significantly increase your earnings. For example, let's say you met your income goal of $100,000 in your first year by closing 100 of 200 sales attempts—a 50% conversion rate. If, in the following year, you made the same amount of sales attempts (200) but increased your conversion rate to 60% by improving your prospecting skills, you would increase your income by 20%. It would look like this:

1st year: 50% conversion x 200 sales attempts = 100 sales

1st year: $100,000 annual income

2nd year: 60% conversion x 200 sales attempts = 120 sales

2nd year: $120,000 annual income

The inherent value in the Law of the Bull's-eye is that by taking better aim at the right prospects, you can increase your earnings without increasing your hours. But securing your business plan is just the beginning of the preparation process for bull's-eye prospecting. While it's important that you establish your numbers up front so you can build an efficient prospecting plan, you still need to determine how to go about making the plan work, or in bull's-eye terms how to take the arrows from your plan and place them in the bow.

> **The inherent value in the Law of the Bull's-eye is that by taking better aim at the right prospects, you can increase your earnings without increasing your hours.**

AIM . . .

The next step in prospecting preparation is determining what sources you have available to you that will increase your prospecting numbers without increasing your time. This step is the equivalent of taking aim at your target.

Step #2: Secure your prospecting sources. There are two types of relationships from which you can draw more prospects without adding hours to your time: those that refer quality prospects to you and those with whom you have partnered for the purpose of gaining referrals and repeat business. The first are called "centers-of-influence." The second are typically existing clients.

Centers-of-influence examples:

> ➤ If you sell medical equipment—a physician who will refer you to departments in the hospital that could buy additional equipment from you

> ➤ If you provide software or network solutions—the CEO of a company who will refer you to Purchasing and IT departments, as well as to other CEOs with Purchasing and IT departments who could purchase additional software and network solutions from you

> ➤ If you are a mortgage lender—a title representative who will refer you to builders and real estate agents who could pass you additional business

> ➤ If you are a car salesperson—a sales manager who will refer you to his sales force, which could contain several people who are in the market for a car

Client Examples:

> If you sell medical equipment—a specific hospital department that needs equipment six or more times per year

> If you provide software or network solutions—a Purchasing and IT department that needs your products and services every single month

> If you are a mortgage lender—a real estate agent whom you currently partner with that refers to you as many as twenty to thirty people each year who need home loans

> If you are a car salesperson—someone on a sales force that you currently have access to who wants a new car for his wife in six months and his son in twelve months

Before you release an arrow at your prospecting target, it's important that you do all you can to increase your probability for landing a long-term, high trust client. That's the reason centers-of-influence are so valuable—because they can save you time and trouble by helping you learn more about your prospects before you try to make them clients. In essence, they're like another archer standing over your shoulder telling you when and when not to release an arrow.

The key to securing your prospecting sources is to ask this question: *Who do I know who knows who I want to know?* Your answer to this question will save you hours of heartache and headache because it will give you your best shot at hitting a bull's-eye. Remember that others can sell you better than you can sell yourself. Therefore, prospecting by referral is the most effective and efficient way to obtain solid sales leads. By using this method you will experience less reluctance in your approach to prospects and higher conversion afterward.

The key to referral prospecting is implementing something I call a "Referral by Design" process, which begins with a script that you use when calling or writing to your prospect sources. The script starts something like this: "I am expanding the sphere and scope of my business and I need your assistance. Whom do you know who . . . ?"

EXAMPLES: Whom do you know who . . .

- ➤ will be buying or selling a home in the next six months?

- ➤ is in need of some financial planning advice?

- ➤ might be in the market for a new car in the next ninety days?

- ➤ is not happy in his regular job and would like to build his own direct sales business?

- ➤ makes decisions regarding his or her company's office supplies?

- ➤ is in charge of purchasing computer equipment for his or her company?

- ➤ will be building a custom home in the next twelve months?

As you customize these for your specific industry, always remember the idea of social proof. Since other people can sell you better than you can, ask your prospecting sources if you can use their names in the body of your approach letters (we'll discuss these shortly) as well as in your appointment-setting process. You will find that in many cases, a prospecting source will agree to make a call for you to help set up an appointment.

The following are brief summaries of five additional methods for obtaining prospect referrals. You should be using each one—as they apply to your industry—to maximize your prospect numbers before shooting for the target:

1. **Point of Sale:** Never leave a successful business development appointment without seeking referrals.

2. **Repurchase Cycles:** If you work with clients that have routine buying cycles, always track them. Never leave a

successful business development appointment or let existing client relationships exist without determining the next order cycle and/or seeking referrals.

3. **Associations/Networking Groups:** Every salesperson should be involved in several associations and networking groups in order to broaden sales and partnership opportunities.

4. **Clubs:** Become known in the organizations in which you are involved. If you are not involved in any, start today. The referrals are there for the taking.

5. **Affinity Businesses:** The word *affinity* means "closely related," and it is very likely that prospects you are converting to clients have other businesses that their primary business is closely related to. Here's a great exercise: Draw a circle in the middle of a sheet of paper and write in that circle your primary client profile. Then in five minutes or less, write every single type of business/prospect that client may be able to refer you to. The first time I did this, it produced ninety-nine additional prospect sources.

Step #3: Check 'em out. After you've secured the best sources from which you will obtain bull's-eye prospects, there's one final step you need to take before you start shooting for the target. In short, you must know who it is you aim to do business with, and then hold your prospects up to that target. Do whatever you can to make sure a prospect you are thinking about pursuing has the potential to become the type of client you want for life. If prospects are going to provide you business over an extended period of time, you need to have a good sense that you will work well together. Your prospect sources can provide a lot of help in this area.

I remember contacting one of my centers-of-influence prior to contacting a prospect. I simply asked her what she knew about my prospect, thinking I would gain some information that would help me better meet this prospect's needs. "Don't!" was her reply. "We have worked with her on and off over the last several years and she is a pain. Save yourself the headaches." My center-of-influence was as instrumental in telling me who *not* to do business with as she was in telling me who *to* do business with.

FIRE!

If to the best of your knowledge your prospects check out, then you're just about ready to begin shooting for the target. But first, you need to make sure your arrows are sharp.

Step #4: Design and send your approach letter. Selling is about building trust, and if prospects don't sense that you are trustworthy in your prospecting initiatives they will never agree to an appointment. That's why it's critical that you sharpen your initial communication with prospects to a fine point.

I've found that a relationship with a prospect usually gets off in the right direction when it begins with an unassuming approach letter. An effective approach letter is a catchy, concise, and cordial one-page introduction that aims to accomplish the following:

> ➢ Captures their attention in the *first paragraph.*

> ➢ Tells them who you are in the *second paragraph.*

> ➢ Lets them know how you got their names in the *third paragraph.* (Use the name of your referral source here.)

> ➢ Piques their interest with a Unique Value Proposition in the *third paragraph.* (I recommend using bullets or something similar to make the U.V.P. easy to see and read.) There are three ingredients to an effective Unique Value Proposition:

> 1. Providing substantial evidence to set you apart from your competition

> 2. Using it early in a relationship to gain trust with a prospect

3. Adding more value to the client than to you

> Suggests the exclusivity of your offer and seeks the next action in the *fourth paragraph*.

A finely crafted approach letter will evoke a sense of genuine curiosity in your prospects as well as lay the groundwork for trust (especially if you send your letter in a creative, catchy package, like the bright-blue mailing tubes my company uses). And an approach letter is certainly a much less threatening and much more considerate way to proceed with a potential client, which will help open the door of opportunity when you follow up.

Step #5: Follow up. Once your letter or letters are sent out, don't just sit around and wait for the phone to ring. Trust me, it won't. You have to follow up if you're ever going to build a high trust business.

The discipline of following up is critical because it speaks volumes about your credibility and trustworthiness. If you're just starting a sales career, you should be following up on prospects every day. As your business matures, the discipline might decrease to once or twice a week. But regardless of how many prospects you need to follow up on, timing is an important key. I recommend using the "48-Hour Rule," which says that you don't send anything out unless you are prepared to follow up within forty-eight hours (obviously this will not apply if your prospects are out of state or country and won't receive your letter within two days). Put it this way: When a letter goes out, discipline yourself to immediately schedule a forty-eight-hour follow up call.

Step #6: Set the appointment with a powerful, value-added script. Ideally, you will have gained a small measure of trust through your approach letter, but the real test of trustworthiness occurs when you talk with a prospect for the first time. Setting the appointment professionally and effectively requires you to be prepared and to have confidence in what you are saying so you don't waver when you get on the phone. And remember, you're calling prospects to add value to their lives, not to add dollars to your bank account.

The following are eight simple steps for setting an appointment:

1. Call the prospect and professionally introduce yourself, making reference to your approach letter.

2. Convey that your referrer or C.O.I. asked you to call, and introduce the prospect to a possible solution for a need in his life or business.

3. Ask the prospect if he has ninety seconds for you to explain.

4. State the purpose of your call.

5. Ask for a thirty-minute face-to-face appointment to explore the possibilities of partnering together.

6. Ask when a convenient time to meet would be.

7. Confirm the goals of the meeting.

8. Thank the prospect and assure him that it will be time well spent.

Make it your goal to see every prospect that you want as a client face-to-face for at least thirty minutes to build the relationship, establish trust, and secure rapport.

The Final Step: Follow up. If your prospect agrees to the appointment, then the stage is set for your high trust interview and sales presentation. But what happens if you follow all this advice and the prospect does not agree to meet with you? The answer is you follow up. Sometimes it takes time for a prospect to say yes. Now, I'm not going to tell you that you should just keep trying and trying until finally the prospect just gives in because she feels sorry for you. Nor am I suggesting that you drive the prospect crazy by inconsiderate, mind-numbing persistence. But what I am saying is that if the prospect is someone you truly desire as a long-term client, don't give up after your first call. Remember that establishing trust takes time, and sometimes that means adding value without receiving business. I don't recommend that you spend the majority of your prospecting time or money trying to land prospects that are undecided or have declined; but if prospects represent your selling bull's-eye and you believe that you can add more value than what they are receiving, commit to adding value to them for one to two years before you throw in the towel.

> Establishing trust takes time, and sometimes that means adding value without receiving business.

As I shared earlier, one of my best accounts agreed to start giving me business eighteen months after she first said no. But as a result of adding value to her over that period of time, she ended up much more satisfied and better served, and her business generated millions of dollars in sales.

Trust me, when you take the time to create and follow a prospecting system that empowers you to consistently take aim and fire at the best prospects in your field, your sales business will quickly reach greater heights. Take a look at this letter from one of my students who implemented the prospecting process we've just discussed:

Dear Todd,

As you know, Andrea and I attended your conference in Lanai this past summer and your sales school in San Francisco just a few weeks ago.

I started working for a new company in a new city after returning from your conference. I had no contacts and knew no one. I bought a database system and set a goal of targeting the top 15 percent, or sixty-five prospects in my market. Using your system, within two weeks my calendar was booked for individual appointments with twenty-two prospects. We had to delay our mailing, as there were no appointment slots for weeks.

I am very excited about our future and much of it has to do with you. I can't thank you enough.

Make it a great day!

John

I spoke with John just a few weeks later and within eight weeks of completing our High Trust Sales Academy he had met with thirty-seven prospects and landed thirty-three new clients from whom he had already received business. I wanted you to see this letter because it demonstrates the incredible value of an effective prospecting system, especially if your goal is to build a highly trustworthy, highly successful business.

YOU'RE ON YOUR WAY

So far we've discussed how to initiate high trust relationships. Now let's begin talking about how to structure your sales business so that you can properly foster high trust relationships—according to the Law of the Scale.

SALES LEADERSHIP APPLICATION

Have you conveyed what a bull's-eye prospect looks like to your people? If you're the leader, that's your job. Helping your people understand the characteristics of the people your company most desires to serve is part of the vision of your business. It's simple: If your people don't know what type of client they're shooting for, you can't expect them to hit the target on a regular basis. Really, you shouldn't expect them to hit it at all.

Take the time to paint a clear portrait of what a bull's-eye client looks, acts, and thinks like. Then help your people aim their sales efforts at that target and nothing else. Doing so will not only release some of their stress, but it will also help your people eliminate some of the frustrations that result from trying to sell to the wrong people.

CHAPTER

TEN

The Law of the Scale

*If You Want More Business,
Have Fewer Clients*

As a young salesperson, I fell victim to it. And as a budding sales professional, you probably did too. In fact, you may still be victim to what is perhaps the most common mistake in the sales profession: trying to meet the needs of everyone while failing to secure the loyalty of anyone.

How many clients have been with you for more than five years? How about ten years? Think about it, because the answers to those questions are very significant when it comes to high trust selling success. The bottom line is that if you're spread too thin to do what is necessary to earn a client's loyalty for life, you're selling yourself short, no pun intended. The Law of the Scale says that if you invest yourself wholly in a few key clients, you will do more business in the long run than if you try to manage the whims of every potential customer. That's because loyal clients reap more revenue and more referrals than one-time customers ever will—even if the numbers are unbalanced.

At one point in Tim Broadhurst's career as a mortgage loan originator, he called thirty real estate agents his clients. He spent time each month fostering relationships with those thirty agents, sending business to them and managing business received from them. During that period of time Tim averaged about $10 million in loan sales a year for two years in a row. Not bad. Tim was making a decent living for himself and his young family, but he hadn't yet applied the Law of the Scale to his business, and therefore wasn't even close to realizing his potential.

153

When Tim finally recognized that he was spreading himself too thin—so much that he couldn't invest the amount of time and energy that his best clients needed or deserved—he cut his clientele by nearly two-thirds. Instead of investing his resources in thirty clients, he began investing all his time and energy in high trust relationships with his top twelve clients. The results speak for themselves. Tim's business quadrupled to $40 million in the first nine months after applying the Law. Not only that, but as an added bonus his time off increased from one week a year to fifteen weeks a year for the next three years. And today Tim's business is still a hot commodity. In fact, he's had to expand his staff to accommodate all the new business that his twelve best clients have brought him, which is now in excess of $80 million a year. And remember that all this happened in less than four years. And all was a result of applying the Law of the Scale.

True victory in the sales profession comes as a result of not only giving people a reason to buy from you, but also making sure they never forget you.

Contrary to what you might think or what you've been taught, it's not enough to just do good business leading up to the sales transaction. Victory is not just in convincing a customer to do business with you *once*. Yes, a good impression and presentation are essential to sales success. But even if you're the most respectable, most knowledgeable, most helpful sales professional leading up to the sale, and you fail to invest in a person after the sale, that customer will forget you more than half of the time. That's a fact. True victory in the sales profession comes as a result of not only giving people a reason to buy from you, but also making sure they never forget you. It's doing more for them after the sale than you did to get the sale. It's the essence of the Law of the Scale.

THE SALES SCALE

Imagine an old-fashioned beam scale, with its brass base and neck, iron beam balanced across the top, and two matching pans hanging off each end of the beam. Imagine that on one side of the scale are two items:

1. the monetary value of a sale, and

2. the endorsement value of a sale, which includes any future business from a sale—repeat or referral.

On the other side of the scale are two items that counter the weight of your sales:

1. financial obligations (personal and professional), and

2. negative sales experiences, which include any customer interaction that results in a loss of future business.

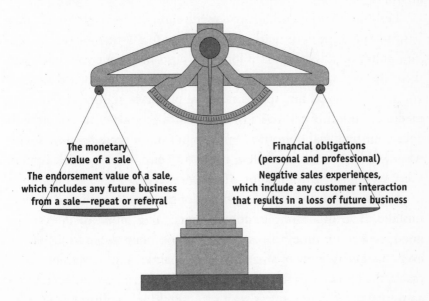

Now, let's say that the weight of a financial obligation is basically the same as the weight of a monetary value of a sale. In other words, if you invest as much money as you make on a sale, the two items balance each other out. With the scale balanced, your success is mediocre at best. You make sales, but your returns are counterbalanced by your investments.

Let's also say that the weight of a negative sales experience is roughly the same as the weight of a positive endorsement from a sale. Or in other words, if you lose as much business from a sale as you gain, the scale will remain balanced. And again, if the scale remains balanced, your business will never take off because you are losing as much business as you are gaining.

Therefore, to be a successful sales professional is to keep the scale tipped in your favor. It is the know-how and ability to continually add more "weight" to the positive side of the scale—to earn more revenue from sales than you invest in getting sales and to acquire more allies than adversaries from sales experiences. Unfortunately, that's often not the case.

Consider the following scenario to help illustrate the Sales Scale at work:

Let's say that last month you made three "midweight" sales that basically paid for your marketing efforts with a little money left over. You didn't do anything extra for those customers, but you didn't rub them the wrong way either, so they were neither compelled to send you more business nor spread negative publicity about you. In all, a mediocre month since you just made enough money to counterbalance your financial obligations and go out to dinner a few times with what was left over. Nonetheless, the month ends with the scale tipping every so slightly in your favor. *Mediocre success.*

Unfortunately, near the beginning of the next month you made a mistake. You made one customer angry. You failed to deliver the goods to him on time because you were too busy trying to juggle the ever-changing whims of two other high-maintenance customers. As a result, the upset customer told five people (that would have been referrals) to avoid doing business with you. *Ouch!* In an effort to juggle all the uncertain business you could handle, you ended up losing the business of at least six people, maybe more. As a result, the next month ends with the scale tipping in the wrong direction.

But let's say that you decide to learn from your mistake by not spending so much time on the revolving door of uncertain sales. Instead you invest more time and money in ascertaining consistent business from your best clients. At the start of the third month, you make a list of the five clients with whom you recently had a good selling experience; then develop a strategy to foster deeper relationships with them. As a result, the scale tips in the wrong direction for the next three months, because you are investing the majority of your resources in securing the loyalty of your top five clients. Nevertheless, you stick with it because you're interested in consistent, lasting success.

In the sixth month your investment strategy pays off. Two of your five best clients bring their business to you again. Not only that, two more of your top five clients refer new business to you. As a result, the sixth month ends with the scale tipping back in your favor. *You're onto something, and you continue to run with it.* The seventh, eighth, and ninth months fare about the same as the sixth, keeping the scale tilted in the right direction. But more importantly, you continue to build stronger, high trust relationships with your best clients, receiving repeat business and acquiring new referrals from them.

By the tenth month, you have secured strong relationships with your top five clients and have also added five referred clients to your list, bringing your high trust client list to ten. After some calculating you estimate that each of your ten clients will average six transactions per year of their own and refer to you six additional transactions from friends or family.

For the rest of that year, you play out your hand by continuing to invest in your ten best clients and assessing your calculations. They turn out to be right on target. You determine that if all you do in the next year is focus the majority of your time on meeting the needs of your top ten clients and their referrals, you can expect a total of about 120 sales transactions or ten per month, which is over three times more than your production from the first month of the previous year. All a result of a change in your selling philosophy.

WEIGHING YOUR SALES SUCCESS

Now, I know what you might be thinking. *That's just fiction. It doesn't happen that way in the real world of sales.* While I'll admit that the story is a fictitious one, the outcome is very realistic. The Law of the Scale is accurate and reliable. And chances are very good that if you're not following the Law in your business, you're not even close to maximizing your sales potential.

Consider one of our clients, Sarah Middleton, who at one point in her sales career produced annual revenue of $115 million with over 250 clients. She was doing well, but didn't have much time for enjoying the fruits of her labor, for living. After receiving coaching from Building Champions on how to apply the Law of the Scale, she decreased her client base from 250 to 50. And guess what? *Her volume stayed exactly the same.* For Sarah, the results are as equally phenomenal as Tim's from the beginning of the chapter. While Sarah did not increase her revenue, she maintained it with 80 percent fewer customers, and as she will quickly tell you, 100 percent fewer headaches. For many of you that may be much more alluring than the money.

At some point (and now is that point if you haven't reached it already) you have to ask yourself, *Why wouldn't I want to increase my income, increase my free time, and decrease my stress?* I don't know a sales professional who doesn't want those things. And the fact is that all three things can become a reality if you put the Law of the Scale into practice. That begins by taking an honest inventory of your current sales relationships.

How have you been treating customers? If you're like most, you may have become accustomed to a "show and blow" methodology. Like a gardener, do you show up, provide your service, then leave before anyone gets home? Do you do a clean job, but offer no real interaction, no real investment because you're more concerned about productivity than people? Do you have some customers who have never even seen you? If so, it's time to make a change.

Just the other day I was in a drugstore and a salesperson said to his buyer, "I'm sorry I haven't been around as often as I'd like. I should try to see you more often." To this the buyer said, "It would

THE LAW OF THE SCALE

probably be good for your sales." That buyer understands the significance of the Law of the Scale. Unfortunately, the salesperson did not, and I don't want you to share in his plight.

> **If nothing sets you apart from your competition,**
> **your clients will always remain someone else's prospects.**

There are a couple of problems with a "show and blow" selling methodology. The first and most obvious is that you are constantly dependent on potential customers for business. That usually proves to be extremely stressful because it's both inconsistent and unpredictable. We've all been there, and I don't think anyone really likes living that way. The second problem with showing and blowing is that when you have no real interaction with your customers outside of what is expected, those customers will not be compelled to use you again or refer you to others. As I said before, a good impression is important, and it may seal one deal for you, but it won't necessarily secure anything beyond the original sale if that's all you do. Put it this way: If nothing sets you apart from your competition, your clients will always remain someone else's prospects.

How does your sales business measure up? If you weighed your current business on the sales scale, which way would it tip? Are your earnings outweighing your financial obligations, or is it an even measurement each month? Are your clients' endorsements adding significant weight to the scale, tipping it consistently in your favor, or do you have as many good sales experiences as bad? If you've never weighed your sales success, do it now. And while our imaginary scale may not provide a precise measurement, it does prove an important point. If you're investing your resources in juggling all the sales you can handle, the scale may or may not tip in your favor—most often not. But when you primarily invest your resources in retaining the high trust and support of your best clients, your actions will eventually tip the scale in your favor for good.

A Movie-Star Approach to Sales

The popular 1996 film *Jerry Maguire* offers a great depiction of a sales professional's discovery and attempt to apply the principles of the Law of the Scale. The opening scene says it all.

Jerry Maguire (played by Tom Cruise) is a professional sports agent who at thirty-five years old has come to the realization that he can no longer stand himself. He has become the lying, schmoozing, money-hungry scrapper he has always despised. With seventy-two different professional athletes as his clients, and an average of 264 phone calls a day, he no longer has time to meet, let alone think about, the real needs of his clients. He has become concerned about one thing and one thing only: the bottom line. And that has finally made him sick. As the movie begins, the narrator (Maguire) conveys to the audience how he finally reached the breaking point.

I'll be honest with you; I started noticing a few years ago and didn't say a word. In the quest for the big dollar a lot of little things were going wrong. Lately, it's gotten worse. Who had I become? Just another shark in a suit?

Two days later, at our corporate conference in Miami, a breakthrough. Breakdown? Breakthrough. I couldn't escape one simple thought: I hated myself. No, no, no, here's what it was: I hated my place in the world.

I had so much to say and no one to listen. And then it happened. It was the oddest, most unexpected thing. I began writing what they call a "mission statement." Not a memo. A mission statement. You know, a suggestion for the future of our company. A night like this doesn't come along very often. I seized it.

What started out as one page became twenty-five. Suddenly, I was my father's son again. I was remembering the simple pleasures of this job. How I ended up here out of law school. The way a stadium sounds when one of my players performs well on the field. The way we are meant to protect them in health, and in injury. With so many clients we had forgotten what was important.

I wrote and wrote and wrote and wrote. And I'm not even a

writer. I was remembering even the words of the original sports agent, my mentor, the late, great Dickey Fox, who said, "The key to this business is personal relationships." Suddenly it was all pretty clear. The answer was fewer clients. Less money. More attention. Caring for them. Caring for ourselves, and the games too. Just starting our lives. Really.

Hey, I'll be first to admit it. What I was writing was somewhat touchy-feely. I didn't care. I had lost the ability to BS. It was the me I'd always wanted to be.

I took it in a bag to a Copymat in the middle of the night and printed up 110 copies. Even the cover looked like the *Catcher in the Rye*. I entitled it: "The Things We Think and Do Not Say: The Future of Our Business." Everyone got a copy.

I was 35. I had started my life.

If you've seen the film, you know that Maguire is fired shortly after distributing his "mission statement" by his boss, Bob Sugar (played by Jay Mohr), who quickly becomes his antagonist. In an awkward-but-passionate display, Maguire vows to the people of his former company that he will succeed despite them. And with the one employee who is inspired by his new mission (Renée Zellweger), he fights against the grain of his profession and his own poor practices to implement his new philosophy.

In one of the final scenes of the movie, we witness Maguire, with tears in his eyes, embracing his only client (Cuba Gooding Jr.), who has just played the football game of his life. Meanwhile, looking on is one of Bob Sugar's clients, who turns to Sugar with a look of concern and says, "Why don't we have a relationship like that?"

SCALING DOWN FOR SUCCESS

Where are you in your quest for sales success? How do you weigh in? How would your clients say you're doing? Are you building high trust relationships or are you just doing business? Maybe, like Jerry Maguire, in the rat race to increase the bottom line you've forgotten the simple pleasures of your job? The close interaction with people?

Seeing the smile on the face of a satisfied customer? Shaking the hand of someone who is more than a client—he's also a good friend? Being genuinely fulfilled at the end of the day because you've added substantial value to clients' lives?

Or maybe, like my friend Tim, you're just spread too thin, and there's no more you can do.

Only you know how your sales business currently weighs in. And only you know whether you're truly applying the Law of the Scale. But regardless of how you measure up right now, if you sense there's still more you can do for others and for yourself, then commit to take the following steps to make the Law of the Scale alive in your business.

Step 1: Take an honest inventory. Even if you're successful now, that doesn't mean you're maximizing your potential. In fact, if you're not living the Law of the Scale, you're probably spending more time than you need to on your job, and producing less than you truly can. To take inventory, simply be honest with yourself. Ask: Do I really know my clients? Do I spend more time building loyal relationships with my best clients or trying to please capricious customers? When was the last time I sat down with my key clients and did a thorough needs analysis and values inventory? Do I have Annual Client Planning sessions to map out the year to come and their future expectations? What percentage of my business comes as a result of repeat sales? Referrals? Am I investing my resources in dependable business from loyal clients or erratic business from arbitrary clients? Honest answers to those and other similar questions will help determine whether you're truly following the Law of the Scale.

Step 2: Measure your productivity over the next month on the sales scale. Are your financial obligations so big that you're outspending your earnings? Are your negative sales experiences outweighing your endorsements? If you weighed the next three months on the scale, would it remain tipped in the same direction or would it seesaw back and forth? If the scale is consistently tipping in the wrong direction or seesawing back and forth, determine what needs to be done to add more weight to the right side of the scale. And remember that the weightiest items are endorsements from satisfied clients that lead to more business.

Step 3: Determine the maximum number of clients you can invest in and still give each the time and energy they deserve. (Take into consideration that these "top" clients will ideally refer you new business as well as bring you their own. Also make sure you factor in the amount of time it will take to receive and manage the referred business.) Remember that your goal is to build long-standing, loyal relationships with these clients. And keep in mind that the best clients may not currently be your clients. Don't just limit yourself to the scope of the clients you've done business with in the past. You may need to start from scratch with some new clients, which includes the clients you can win from your competition through the Law of the Bull's-eye.

Step 4: Begin investing in your top clients today. Don't wait until they come to you. Come up with creative ways to reach out to them. Share your vision with them—the vast majority of the people you serve would be thrilled with the prospect of being one of your most valued clients. You may even want to consider coming up with some sort of agreement with them whereby you consent to offer them ongoing "Premium Services" for their promise of a decided amount of both future business and referral business. Both Tim and Sarah, my clients whose stories I shared earlier in the chapter, did this with great success.

Step 5: Be patient. Don't get down on yourself if in the first few months you don't see a major difference. Remember that you are changing the way you do business, and it may take some time to do so—especially if you're building your top clients list from scratch. I'm not going to tell you that you have to make the change cold turkey. Only you know the sacrifices you are able to make and still stay afloat. But understand this: The sooner you establish the Law of the Scale in your business, the sooner you will realize a level of sales success that you never thought possible. I strongly encourage you to do whatever it takes to implement the Law as soon as possible, even sooner. Trust me when I say that any sacrifice you make will be well worth it. Because the Law of the Scale will dramatically improve more than your business; it will improve your way of life.

SALES LEADERSHIP APPLICATION

If you are leading a sales force, you need to evaluate how to best empower your current and future salespeople to implement the Law of the Scale individually. I recommend following the lead of one of my company's clients, Rich Land, who runs a sales force of fifty-eight salespeople. He increased his per-rep productivity by 300 percent in less than a year by applying the Law across the board to his recruiting, training, and ongoing development strategy. By doing this, he made sure every person on his sales force was continually empowered for personal and corporate success. Taking these steps may require that you restructure how your people are compensated for their sales. And it may result in some people leaving the company. But regardless of what you must do, or what occurs as a result, implementing the Law of the Scale for your team is a must for maximum, consistent success.

CHAPTER ELEVEN

The Law of Courtship

For a Relationship to Be Right on the Outside,
It Must First Be Right on the Inside

O ne thing everyone can identify with is dating. Why do people date? I think you'd agree that, generally speaking, dating is for the purpose of learning as much as possible about a person to determine whether there is good reason to invest in a more intimate relationship. And if the dating process continues in good faith, its purpose is also to prepare those involved for a healthy, lifelong marriage.

The truth is that without a sufficient period of dating, many traditional marriages in Western culture—those not arranged by family—tend to be short-lived, because there is much about the other person that remains unknown. There is much that may yet prove to be untrustworthy. Such whimsical marriages tend to stand on precarious commitments, and fall on the same. Recent history has shown, especially in the U.S., that the success of such marriages is hopeful at best, but certainly not probable. And a relationship with a customer will follow the same path.

> **Sales professionals would increase their success rates dramatically if they did a better job of "dating" their prospects before ever saying "I do" to a sales relationship.**

Sales professionals would increase their success rates dramatically if they did a better job of "dating" their prospects before ever saying "I do" to a sales relationship. But the problem is that most salespeople rush into a commitment without knowing anything substantial about a person. Without knowing whether there are shared values and shared goals. Without knowing the others' expectations, needs, or desires. As a result, like a whimsical marriage, the success of such relationships is shaky at best.

Before I understood the Law of Courtship, my approach was something like, "Get the prospects you can, take the business you can, and make the money you can." Using this so-called strategy, I managed to do some business but soon found myself in a maze of problems. The phone was ringing more than ever, with clients on the other end placing demands on me that were unrealistic. Before long, I was nearly always the bad guy. I started receiving threats like, "If you don't do this for me, I will never give you another order for as long as you live." Tough language. I started responding—in the wrong way. I started compromising my standards for how I would handle relationships. I began allowing clients do whatever they wanted so I could keep their business. I was violating a code of conduct, which had been established in me since I was a young boy. And my clients, I was learning, did not share some of these same ideals. Things like professionalism, integrity, courtesy, and quality.

As I watched my business spin out of control, I found that the longer I took business from these customers, the worse I felt about me, and the more I put my longevity as a sales professional into jeopardy. Things didn't ever get any better until I decided to make things better. Eventually I learned that much of what was important to many of my clients wasn't important to me—and I could have learned that early on, even before I started taking orders from them.

The Law of Courtship says that for a sales relationship to work on the outside, it must first be right on the inside. In other words, for you to build loyal, lasting relationships with your clients, you must take the time to know them, not just know *about* them. And you must allow them to know you. The Law of Courtship is about dating a prospect before you propose a sales marriage. You see, the more you know your prospects—what's important to them about a relationship with you, what they look for in your product or service, and what they place value on—the more competent and confident you are to make a decision about pursuing a deeper, more meaningful relationship.

RELATIONSHIPS MUST BE "ESSENTIAL"

Last year, as I was boarding the American Airlines tram in Dallas, I saw Ken Blanchard and stopped to say hello. I learned that he was also headed home on the same flight to San Diego where we both live. We managed to conduct a little on-board seat negotiation so we could sit together for the two-and-a-half-hour flight. What I thought was going to be a casual conversation turned into a much-needed time of professional growth. I think you, too, will learn a lot from what we discussed.

> **Relationships have two parts—essence and form. If essence is wrong, you will spend 90 percent of your time on form.**

At the time, I was suffering from some serious anxiety about one of my business relationships and wasn't quite sure how to handle it. In fact, I had just come from Atlanta, where I had brought my concerns about the relationship to a good friend. He was very clear that I needed to make some changes. So as I shared with Ken this same concern, he listened, then reminded me of something I had overlooked: Relationships have two parts—essence and form. If essence is wrong, you will spend 90 percent of your time on form.

Ken's explanation exposes the root of most failing or failed sales relationships, including my own at that time. The seed of relationship troubles is planted when salespeople try to build revenue before building relationships, or in other words, pursue marriage without dating. They try to grow the outside of relationships (the form) before cultivating the inside of relationships (the essence). And the result is that most sales relationships end up very shallow and thus very fruitless.

Every business relationship, personal or professional, is governed by this same principle. In new sales relationships, every prospect will either have an essence match with you or they will not, just like dating. If there is a shared essence, the relationship can be highly profitable and void of unreasonable demands and stress, just like a successful marriage. However, if you and a customer do not have a shared essence, the relationship will suffer under a burden of unrealistic expectations and unneeded stress, like a troubled marriage. Part of your job as a sales professional is to consciously decide what type of relationships you want your business founded on, then stick with that standard.

For example, let's say that you are a real estate agent selling homes for a living. Generally speaking, your clients will obviously be those who desire to sell their homes—and that's where the relationship standards for most real estate agents end. But the most successful agents establish much higher and more specific standards because they want the highest return for the investment of their time and resources. If you desired to be highly successful as a real estate agent, and eliminate unnecessary stress within your client relationships, you would need to do the same. And that will mean turning down business from those clients or potential clients who don't meet your standards.

For instance, let's say that your neighbor three houses down sends a co-worker to you who wants to sell his home in the next two months. Because he's a friend of a friend, you agree to meet with him once in order to determine whether there is potential for a strong relationship. You agree to one "date," so to speak. But in that first meeting, you learn that your neighbor's colleague holds an unrealistic opinion of the value of his home, which he's firmly set on; and what's worse is that his home is showing signs of termite infestation—something he wants you to try and keep "under wraps" or at least "downplay" as much as possible. Clearly, integrity is not high on his list—if on his list at all—and he shows signs of being somewhat obtuse and self-serving. In all, not someone with whom you'd enjoy doing business—not even once. And while you could do what most people in the real estate industry do and follow through with the sale in order to make a few bucks, you'd be wasting your time in doing so. You'd be not only compromising your own client standards—assuming you had set them—you'd also be investing time in a high-maintenance relationship that offers no real potential for high returns. Therefore, you would be taking away from time that could be invested in a highly enjoyable, highly profitable relationship.

ASKING FOR SALES SUCCESS

Following the Law of Courtship is not complicated. To do so you must simply discipline yourself to take the steps necessary to determine whether a relationship has a high probability for lasting success before going any further. Confidence in the future success of a relationship comes when a shared essence has been established—when both parties knowingly share the same values, expectations, and desires for the relationship—something that was clearly lacking in our illustration. In short, the key to the Law of Courtship is making sure that before you get deeply involved with a person, you know with whom you are getting involved. It's making sure the relationship is right on the inside first, where it matters most, and only then pursuing it further.

Once you've sufficiently mastered prospecting and appointment setting, the next most important skill set in the high trust selling process is the ability to pose meaningful questions to those with whom you're considering a relationship. Sometimes, as in our previous illustration, a prospect's answers are evident without asking questions. But that's not usually the case and shouldn't be counted on. Like a dating relationship, your goal in asking questions is to learn your prospects' values, needs, desires, and expectations so you can determine if there is enough in common on the inside to continue. Unfortunately, most salespeople fail miserably in this arena. The reasons are simple: They either don't care enough to ask, or they don't know what to ask. Either way, they skip a very important part of developing a high trust relationship. Think of it this way: If you wouldn't marry someone you don't know anything about, you shouldn't do business with someone you don't know either. Furthermore, you shouldn't expect business from someone who doesn't know you.

In every piece of research my company has conducted, every live field call on which we have gone, every observation between buyer and seller that we have made, the ability to ask meaningful, well-thought-out questions has been integral for establishing a lasting, lucrative sales relationship. In fact, every successful salesperson we have observed, coached, and/or tracked has demonstrated that he or she

> ➢ has questions written and thought out in advance of meeting with a prospect
> ➢ has a protocol for how and when to ask questions
> ➢ has a different questioning process for determining the potential of a relationship than for securing and sustaining a relationship
> ➢ has an ongoing questioning process to ensure client satisfaction and relationship growth
> ➢ asks questions for the purpose of customizing solutions
> ➢ asks questions for the purpose of meeting needs

And for you to establish lasting relationships in your sales career, you, too, must acquire a knack for asking the right questions of your prospects—even if that means asking them about something with which you are not entirely comfortable. In our illustration, it might have become necessary to question the prospect about his desire to hide the potential termite problem or ask him to explain the seemingly steep valuation he places on his home.

The importance of asking questions is obvious when you consider that all prospects have values they want considered, needs they want met, objectives they want accomplished, and perhaps dreams they want fulfilled, all in the context of their buying strategies. Ideally, your product or service should meet each of these conditions, but if it doesn't or can't, you're wasting your time trying to sell. In fact, attempting to foster a sales relationship despite an essence mismatch is like trying to get a date with someone who's not remotely interested in you. It's just not going to happen—or if it does, it's predicated on propaganda or pity, which never last. Asking the right questions ensures that such unenviable outcomes don't occur. The right questions—and an actively listening ear—will help you understand prospects' core values and real needs, ideally putting you in a position to add value with your product where value is both wanted and needed most.

PUTTING IT ALL TOGETHER: THE HIGH TRUST INTERVIEW

The trust bond between you and your prospects is the absolute foundation for profitable, long-term relationships. All the sales training in the world will not create lasting success if your prospects don't trust you. But as trust goes up, tension goes down, and acceptance of your proposition increases. Take a look at the following chart.

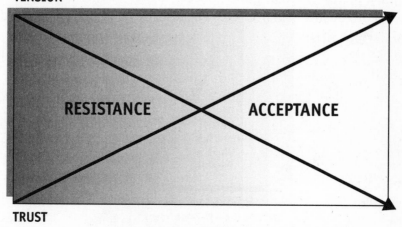

TENSION

RESISTANCE   ACCEPTANCE

TRUST

ACTIONS OVER TIME

As you can see, sales interactions generally begin with high tension and low trust, which results in resistance to your proposition. But as you move your prospects from low to high trust, their tension decreases and the likelihood of their acceptance increases.

> The trust bond between you and your prospects is the absolute foundation for profitable, long-term relationships. All the sales training in the world will not create lasting success if your prospects don't trust you.

There is an effective procedure by which you can accomplish this called the High Trust Interview. It's the embodiment of the Law of Courtship, and once implemented and mastered, it will give you the means to effectively build the high trust relationships necessary for substantial sales success. But before we begin discussing the first step in the high trust interview, I want to do a quick review of what we've discussed thus far in Section II to make sure you understand where the Law of Courtship fits into the big picture of high trust selling success.

If you remember, in Chapter 8—the Law of the Dress Rehearsal—we talked about the importance of being well prepared for every selling interaction. That included a brief explanation of the High Trust Selling System (HTSS), which outlines the four major Acts you must master to build a high trust sales business. Here's a snapshot reminder of the four Acts:

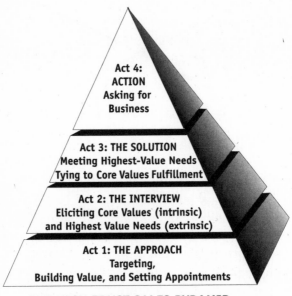

Act 4:
ACTION
Asking for
Business

Act 3: THE SOLUTION
Meeting Highest-Value Needs
Tying to Core Values Fulfillment

Act 2: THE INTERVIEW
Eliciting Core Values (intrinsic)
and Highest Value Needs (extrinsic)

Act 1: THE APPROACH
Targeting,
Building Value, and Setting Appointments

THE HIGH TRUST SALES PYRAMID

You'll recall that Act 1 (your approach) centers on determining who you will and will not do business with. We addressed the application of Act 1 in the previous two chapters. The Law of the Bull's-eye taught you how to aim for the best prospects to build your new business or expand your existing business; and the Law of the Scale taught you how to reprioritize your current client base to ensure that you are only building your business on a lasting foundation of the most loyal and lucrative clients. That brings us to Act 2 (the interview) of the High Trust Selling System.

You'll recall that Act 2 (your interview) centers on how to create high trust with new sales prospects. It is this Act that sales professionals are prone to skip more than any other because they get greedy or overanxious. Therefore, Act 2 in the High Trust Selling System is the first key to setting yourself apart from the run-of-the-mill competition and elevating your business to an elite level. And Act 2 begins when you learn to apply the Law of Courtship. More specifically, when you learn to conduct a high trust interview (HTI) with your top sales prospects. Let's begin now with the first step.

THE HIGH TRUST INTERVIEW

STEP 1: A HIGH-IMPACT OPENING

Without question, when you are meeting with prospects for the first time you need to make an immediate positive impact. First impressions are critical, but unfortunately most salespeople struggle in this area. Whether it's from lack of preparation, lack of confidence, lack of purpose, or a little case of the nerves, most salespeople spend their first few minutes with a prospect increasing tension and decreasing trust. The Law of the Dress Rehearsal hopefully helped you recognize the importance of being well rehearsed before entering a selling situation with a prospect so that you come across in a professional, competent, caring manner. And if you are well rehearsed, you have a much better shot at gaining prospects' trust in the first few minutes of your interview.

The purpose of a high-impact opening is simply to gain permission to ask the questions that will provide the information you need for both determining whether a shared essence exists and offering specific solutions to a prospect's needs. All effective High-Impact Openings have the following characteristics:

1. **An appreciation for the prospect's time.** This is self-explanatory. Too much small talk or time on pleasantries is a surefire sign to a prospect that you're nervous and not prepared. If you've been referred to a prospect, use the referrer's name in your opening. This usually helps secure enough trust to continue the conversation.

2. **A statement of impact.** You must say something that uniquely sets you apart from your competition and foreshadows the value that the conversation will hold if it continues.

3. **A quick transition to the questioning process.** The key here is to maintain control of the dialog by quickly transitioning to Values Discovery Questions and Highest Value Needs Questions.

We'll discuss Values Discovery and Highest Value Needs Questions in a minute. But first let me give you some examples of high-impact openings.

Here's how a high-impact opening might sound if you are selling sales training services:

"Mr. Smith, I really appreciate your time and am thankful that Debbie asked us to get together. A lot of people think I am in the business of selling sales training systems to companies but I really don't see it that way at all. I see my goal as helping my clients achieve the highest level of success possible with effective leadership and sales rep productivity. And my experience has shown me that I can do a better job helping you achieve maximum leadership and sales rep productivity if I know what's important about the success of your training to you. So, Mr. Smith, help me understand: What's important to you about successful sales training systems?"

Here's how a high-impact opening might sound if you are in the office equipment business selling copiers:

"Mr. Smith, I really appreciate your time and am thankful that Debbie asked us to get together. A lot of people think I am in the business of selling copiers to my clients, but I really don't see it that way at all. I see my real goal as helping my clients achieve the highest level of success possible with the copiers they invest in, protecting their images and boosting their quality while minimizing their costs. My experience has shown me that I can do a better job meeting your needs if I know what's important about these issues and the role your copiers play. So, Mr. Smith, help me understand: What's important to you about the copy machines you are considering purchasing?"

Here's how a high-impact opening might sound if you are a financial planner:

"Mr. Smith, I really appreciate your time and am thankful that Debbie asked us to get together. A lot of people think I am in the business of simply creating financial plans, but I really don't see it that way at all. I see my real goal as helping my clients achieve the highest level of financial success possible by helping them integrate an overall plan for managing their money, minimizing their expenses, and maximizing their cash flow. My experience has shown me that I can do a better job meeting your needs if I know what is important about achieving financial success to you. So, Mr. Smith, help me understand: What's important to you about financial success?"

Here's how a high-impact opening might sound if you are a mortgage lender:

"Mr. Smith, I really appreciate your time and am thankful that Debbie asked us to get together. A lot of people think I am in the business of doing loans, but I really don't see it that way at all. I see my primary role as helping my borrowers integrate the mortgage loans they select into their overall long- and short-term financial and investment goals, while also meeting their payment, equity, and cash flow objectives. My experience has shown me that I can do a better job meeting your needs if I know what's important about this home loan to you. So, Mr. Smith, help me understand: What's important to you about this home loan?"

The total time for a high-impact opening should be between forty-five and sixty seconds. Once you've professionally and genuinely conveyed your high-impact opening, you can move on, with the permission of your prospect, to the next step.

STEP 2: VALUES DISCOVERY QUESTIONS (INTRINSIC NEEDS)

While the high-impact opening indicates the importance of first impressions, it is not the most critical step in the high trust interview. That billing belongs to values discovery questions and highest value needs questions because both will do more to sustain buyer interest and create high trust than the most impressive high-impact opening ever will.

> **People buy feelings. Yet most salespeople sell features or benefits, which are almost never effective in relationship-based sales.**

People buy feelings. Yet most salespeople sell features or benefits, which are almost never effective in relationship-based sales. If your goal is to build high trust, a giant step is taken when the features of your product or services are tied to a prospect's intrinsic needs and values. You have no doubt heard sales trainers claim that to get a sale you have to sell to the emotion of the buyer. While that may be true in the end, it's deficient advice. The truth is that the best salespeople simply have a knack for learning what their prospects' fundamental values are (their essence), then selling to those value areas where the deepest emotions exist.

Step 2 in the high trust interview is about asking questions that predictably lead you to your prospects' greatest values as they consider life, business, and a relationship with you. Questions like

- ➢ What's important to you about being successful?
- ➢ What's important to you about earning more money?
- ➢ What's important to you about maximizing your image?
- ➢ What's important to you about productivity?
- ➢ What's important to you about saving money?
- ➢ What's important to you about achieving security?
- ➢ What's important to you about safety?
- ➢ What's important to you about making a difference?
- ➢ What's important to you about saving time?
- ➢ What's important to you about profitability?

When you are selling security, self-image, peace of mind, fulfillment, satisfaction, prestige, happiness, joy, or serenity, a prospect is much more apt to receive your information without excessive resistance.

Here's how Step 2 might sound if you are in the office equipment business selling copiers:

You: So, Mr. Smith, help me understand: What's important to you about the copy machines you are considering purchasing?

Prospect: I want our copy machines to be incredibly durable and able to withstand a ton of use.

You: Great! Our clients all have different things that are important to them in selecting copy machines, and that is one of them. What's important to you about having durable copiers that can withstand a lot of use?

Prospect: I am tired of having frustrated workers complaining about the fact that they can't get their work done every time a copier breaks down. I don't want them to have any excuses.

You: That makes perfect sense. Let me ask you: What's important to you about your employees not having any excuses for getting their work done?

Prospect: Obviously, our overall performance will improve.

You: What's most important to you about improving your overall performance?

Prospect: Having peace of mind in knowing that we are doing our very best.

As you can see, in this example the high trust interview was advanced by the same question with a slightly different slant, depending on the product or service that is offered. The prospect's initial answers were not very emotional but you can see that by inserting each answer back into the next question, you can naturally lead a prospect to sharing his most central values in conducting business with someone like you. It's important to note that beginning with this part of the high trust interview, you should be recording your prospect's answers on a sheet of paper. Don't force yourself to try and remember everything you've been told. As you listen, jot down the prospect's key needs and values so you can continually and accurately reference them as you interview. You may even want to create an HTI form to fill out as you get to know your prospect better.

The total time your values discovery questions should take is three to seven minutes. Then, once you've established a prospect's central values and believe they are in tune with your values, you are ready to move on to the third and final step of the high trust interview.

STEP 3: HIGHEST VALUE NEEDS QUESTIONS (EXTRINSIC NEEDS)

Highest Value Needs are the relational needs and expectations on which the prospect places the highest value. These nearly always have to do with deliverables. Prospects will generally answer highest value needs questions with terms like *quality, speed, professionalism, accessibility, clear communication, knowledge,* and *integrity.* There are many more, but these are the most common. The goal in Step 3 is to learn how prospects expect you to conduct business and maintain the relationship so that you can customize a highly attractive buying strategy. You will generally want to discover between three and five needs.

Here's how you transition from Step 2 to Step 3 if you are selling copiers:

You: Mr. Smith, now that I understand what's important to you about the copy machines you are considering purchasing, what is the most important thing to you about partnering with a professional copier salesperson?

Remember that these questions are generally less about the product and more about the relationship. That's because if a buyer doesn't trust you, your product features are usually insignificant. Make sure you don't get ahead of yourself here. Even if the prospect has shared with you his values and his expectations, that doesn't mean you are equipped to foster a profitable relationship—not yet at least. There is still more you can learn in an efficient manner to set you up for success.

Even though the highest value needs question is answered, you are not through with Step 3 in the high trust interview. Because people define things very differently, you must ensure that you understand what your prospect has told you. There are three steps to this process:

1. Ascertain the need.

2. Understand their rules. (This will help prove you are delivering.)

3. Discover the specific benefit(s) the prospect desires to reap from the need being met.

For every need you hear and record (remember, you're striving for three to five), you must elicit as much information about that need as possible in an efficient and professional manner. This evidence-gathering process will help you customize a needs-specific sales presentation when the time is right. During this process, keep in mind that it's never safe to assume you understand what a prospect is thinking.

Once you ascertain a prospect's need, you must understand the prospect's rules by which those needs will be met by asking questions like:

- ➢ "How do you define . . . ?"
- ➢ "What would you change . . . ?"
- ➢ "How do you determine . . . ?"
- ➢ "What is your past experience with . . . ?"
- ➢ "How would you improve . . . ?"
- ➢ "What does that look like to you?"
- ➢ "What parameters are critical to you for . . . ?"
- ➢ "What have you found works best for . . . ?"
- ➢ "How do you select . . . ?"
- ➢ "What are your standards for . . . ?"

Here is how you would learn the prospects first need and rules.

You: Mr. Smith, now that I understand what's important to you about the copy machines you are considering purchasing, what is the most important thing to you about partnering with a professional copier salesperson?

Prospect: Good communication

You: That's great! Good communication means different things to different people. How do you define good communication?

Prospect: The first thing that comes to mind is honesty. I want to know that what you say will happen is what is going to happen.

You: That's very important. What are some of your other standards for good communication?

Prospect: I like to have my calls returned the same day I call.

You: That's very reasonable. What else?

Prospect: I like to be kept in the loop. I like to have order status updates on a weekly basis.

You: That is obviously critical. I don't want you ever guessing where your orders are. Is there anything else?

Prospect: No, those are the main things relative to communication.

Once you have this information, then you need to simply discover the benefit Mr. Smith is looking to receive as a result of his communication needs being met. To conclude, you would simply say something similar to the following:

You: Mr. Smith, this is very helpful information. Tell me why honest, timely, regular communication is important to you?

Prospect: It gives me peace of mind because it alleviates my worries.

Notice how the ultimate benefit that Mr. Smith seeks from your communication has an emotional feel to it, similar to his values. That's the information you must seek to learn from every prospect on his or her most important needs if you desire to establish a lasting relationship. You see, it's obvious that a copy machine prospect like Mr. Smith would want a copier that is fast, reliable, high quality, and reasonably priced. Very few prospects wouldn't want those things. Therefore, it doesn't set you apart from your competition if you immediately break into a conversation with a prospect by telling him about how your copiers are fast, reliable, of the highest quality, and reasonably priced. You need to be selling more than a really good copier. To be a top-notch salesperson, you need to be selling solutions to your prospects' deepest needs. You need to be selling the fulfillment of your prospects' deepest desires—in Mr. Smith's case, peace of mind.

After completing the above sequence, you will have uncovered one important need of your prospect. But remember that your objective is to ascertain between three and five needs. Therefore to continue the conversation (and your search for more needs), you would simply ask, "Mr. Smith, what else is important to you about partnering with a professional copier salesperson?" Then for the next ten to twenty minutes you will discuss with your prospect all of the needs he has relative to working with you. To effectively develop his buying strategy, you will want to compare the needs as you go to determine which is most important, which is second, and so on. Your goal here is very simple: When you get to Act 3 in the HTSS, The Solution, you will want to present solutions to the prospect's needs in order of his importance to him. For instance, clear, consistent communication may not be Mr. Smith's most important need.

Let's say that as you continue your high trust interview, you discover that problem resolution is actually his most important need, and product training is his third most important need. In this scenario, your buying strategy would then be to present effective solutions to his need for problem resolution first, his need for communication second, and his need for product training last. It's important to note that different prospects have different buying strategies. For example, another copier client may have the same three needs as Mr. Smith but in a different order of importance. In that case you would alter your presentation accordingly.

THE GATEWAY TO SALES

The high trust interview is so successful because it helps you ascertain what you must be selling to gain both the trust and the business of a prospect. But let me be very clear here: Do not go this far with a prospect, and then continue the selling process if you cannot or will not deliver what the prospect desires. Integrity is vital—integrity with yourself and integrity with your prospects. The information that you acquire from a high trust interview is not to be manipulated in any way. If, for revenue's sake, you attempt to be something you are not or try to sell your product as something it is not, you will never make it in the sales profession. Yes, you might make a sale or two that's predicated on deceit. But that kind of selling will burn you. And when it does, you'll be lucky to remain in business.

> **There are enough people that will do business your way to not worry about those who won't.**

The high trust interview is not about learning how to manipulate a prospect. It's about learning how to serve a prospect in the best possible way. It's about meeting real needs, not trying to manufacture phony needs. And if, at any time during the interview process, you recognize that the relationship can never be right on the inside, save yourself the grief and don't pursue it any further. As my friend Jim Rohn says, "There are enough people that will do business your way to not worry about those who won't."

Remember the story I told you earlier in the chapter? The one about me compromising my sales relationship standards in order to keep business? Well, the truth is that nothing changed for me until I learned the value of the high trust interview. But when I began to experiment with this strategy, I started to see good and bad tendencies in business relationships before ever doing business with potential clients. I learned whether we shared the same values and expectations.

In fact, as a result of this learning process, I sat down with some of my existing clients and interviewed them for the first time. It then became abundantly clear to me why my business was suffering—I was letting my clients set the standards and values for my business. No wonder I had such high levels of frustration and stress. I remember one defining instance, not long after making this discovery, when an existing client asked me to do something that I knew was wrong, something that would violate my integrity and quite possibly jeopardize my career. In the past, I had complied with such requests from this particular client, but this time I said no—even though it meant losing business. I knew that I needed to stop my destructive pattern, so I said, "John, over the last several months we have done a lot of business together, and I appreciate it. However, after evaluating my long-term plan, I cannot do for you what you want in a vendor. So rather than modify the way I do business best, I'd like to thank you for your business and recommend you find another vendor who will give you the type of service you desire." That was the end of the story—and I felt great.

On another occasion, I was conducting a high trust interview with a potential client, and as we meandered through the dialogue I became increasingly uncomfortable with his expectations. So rather than pretend his expectations were harmless—as I had done prior to learning the Law of Courtship—I said, "Tom, we have spent about thirty minutes together, and my sense is that what you want from a vendor and what I know I can give you are not the same. So rather than pretend this disparity doesn't exist, I want to thank you for your time and recommend that you continue to search for suppliers that can help you the way you want." I then excused myself from the interview and moved on.

While my actions with Tom may seem a bit abrupt to you, the fact is that such action is not only in *your* best interest, but your prospect's as well. Tom and I were not a good match. That's that. I knew it. And truth be told, he probably did too. Staying together would have only magnified our mismatch and caused unnecessary stress. Therefore, ending it was the best thing for both of us to do.

The central message of the Law of Courtship is getting to know your prospects. For some that might take more than one interview. For others that might take only fifteen minutes. But the implication is the same either way: You must establish whether you and a prospect are right for each other before you ever enter a buyer/seller relationship. High trust selling is about client relationships with long-term commitment and lifelong loyalty. And if you're interested in reaching your potential and being truly fulfilled as a sales professional, those are the relationships by which you must build your business.

As you journey forward to the next chapter, I will show how to take the information that you gathered in your high trust interview and use it to offer compelling sales presentations that have a significant impact on every one of your bull's-eye prospects. You will also learn how to have a competitive advantage in every sales offering, how to effectively manage any objection that surfaces, and how to get prospects who are saying no to say yes, and really mean it.

If you're ready to get down to the nitty-gritty of the high trust selling process, let's start by discussing how to perform Acts 3 and 4 of the High Trust Selling System, which are a part of the Law of the Hook.

SALES LEADERSHIP APPLICATION

As the leader of a sales team, make sure every one of your salespeople understands how to conduct an effective high trust interview. If it's appropriate, hold a team meeting and walk your team through each step of the process, having them practice interacting with one another. You may even want to have copies of Steps 1 through 4 of the interview made for each of your salespeople so that they can post them somewhere near their phones and use them as a guide until conducting a high trust interview becomes second nature.

If following the Law of Courtship is a radical change from the way your company normally conducts business, it's also important that you convey to your people why you are implementing a new strategy and process for selling. Explain to them that your desire is to build a lasting, lucrative sales business for everyone involved, and that requires a change in strategy. While you may experience some resistance at first, make it your goal to empower your salespeople to succeed the right way or not at all. Remember that your job as the leader is to not only set the tone, but also to follow through.

CHAPTER

TWELVE

The Law of the Hook

A Captivated Audience
Stays to the End

Think about the most intriguing book you've read recently. How did the book begin? At what stage were you hooked? There's no doubt something caught your attention right off the bat. Otherwise, you wouldn't have kept turning the pages, staying up half the night trying to finish it. What about a television show or movie that you've seen recently that kept you on the edge of your seat and stirred some real emotions? How did the story open? It was no doubt captivating. Otherwise, your eyes wouldn't have remained glued to the screen. Maybe the hero's wife was killed, and you just had to know if he would find the strength to make it through and maybe even avenge her death. Maybe something completely unexplainable happened and someone, you hoped, would be able to figure out what it all means. Maybe a guy and a girl met and fell in love in some romantic location, but then had to face the reality of living in two very different worlds, three thousand miles away . . . and you had to know if they made it back to each other, somehow.

Now think about your last selling experience. How did it start off? Were you captivating? Did you pique your prospect's interest so that she was compelled to move forward with you? Did you draw out an emotion in her that she truly wanted to feel? Did you create a desire in your prospect to want more of the same experience? If you were following the Law of the Hook, you did all these things and more.

The Law of the Hook says that a captivated audience stays to the end. That's because the principle that keeps your eyes glued to a screen and your hands glued to a book is the same principle that keeps your prospects glued to you. You see, an audience is an audience whether in a sales office or a theater; and to keep an audience around, the performance must be captivating from the get-go. Think about it this way: When was the last time you finished a book that didn't grab you in the first chapter? If you're like me, there are probably several books gathering dust on your shelves that just didn't make the cut because they weren't intriguing enough in the beginning. They didn't grab your attention. And the same is true of salespeople who fail to captivate their audiences in the beginning—they are brushed aside for someone more alluring.

On the other hand, when prospects are captivated by what you offer to them and by the way you offer it, they are compelled to give you their business; and not just once. Quality, high trust salesmanship is like a great book or movie; it captivates right away and keeps one coming back for more.

Consider the following hook from the opening of Louis L'Amour's famous story, *Off the Mangrove Coast:*

> There were four of us there, at the back end of creation, four of the devil's own, and a hard lot by any man's count. We'd come together the way men will when on the beach, the idea cropping up out of an idle conversation. We'd nothing better to do; all of us being fools or worse, so we borrowed a boat of the Nine Islands and headed out to sea.
>
> Did you ever cross the South China Sea in a forty-foot boat during the typhoon season? No picnic certainly, not any job for a churchgoing son; more for the likes of us, who mattered to no one, and in a stolen boat, at that.
>
> Now, all of us were used to playing it alone. We'd worked aboard ship and other places, sharing our labors with other men, but the truth was, each was biding his own thoughts, and watching the others.

There was Limey Johnson, from Liverpool, and Smoke Bassett from Port au Prince, and there was Long Jack from Sydney, and there was me, the youngest of the lot, at loose ends and wandering in a strange land . . .

It was Limey Johnson who told us the story of the freighter sinking off the mangrove coast; a ship with fifty thousand dollars in the captain's safe and nobody who knew it was there anymore . . . nobody but him.

Fifty thousand dollars . . . and we were broke. Fifty thousand lying in a bare ten fathoms, easy for the taking. Fifty thousand split four ways. A nice stake, and a nice bit of money for the girls and the bars in Singapore or Shanghai . . . or maybe Paris.

Twelve thousand five hundred dollars a piece . . . if we all made it. And that was a point to be thought upon, for if only two should live . . . twenty five thousand dollars . . . and who can say what can or cannot happen in the wash of a weedy sea off the mangrove coast? Who can say what is the destiny of any man? Who could say how much some of us were thinking of lending a hand to fate?

Do you want to read on? L'Amour really has you hooked, doesn't he? (It's no coincidence there are more than 260 million copies of his books in print around the world.) Thanks to Louis L'Amour, you're captivated to know what happens to the four salty wanderers. Do they really go for the treasure? Do they find it? Does someone get killed in the process? Is the death an accident or murder? "Who," as L'Amour's character says, "can say what is the destiny of any man?" That question is what's got you hooked. Someone knows the destiny of these four men and you want to know too . . . so you go back for more.

What's your hook? Do you have one? Do you offer your prospects something so intriguing and captivating that they have to know the rest of the story—that they can't wait to see the deal through to the end? If you don't have a hook, it's time you did.

Based on what you initially say, do, hand out, mail out, promote, or distribute to ask for business, can you honestly say that you would be compelled to place an order with you? *Would you be captivated by you?* Would you do business with you based on the impact of your opening performance? If you're not sure, it's time to change the way you sell.

In the previous three chapters we discussed how to perform Acts 1 and 2 of the High Trust Selling System, which lead up to your sales offering. Let's quickly review them here:

ACT 1: THE APPROACH

This is the process by which you predetermine who your best prospects are, and then initiate high trust relationships with them by effectively setting an appointment to meet.

ACT 2: THE INTERVIEW

This is the process that follows your Approach in which you conduct a high trust interview to secure the shared essence between you and your prospects. It is also in this Act that you establish your prospects' needs, their buying strategies, and the emotional fulfillment you must offer in order to meet their real needs and gain their business.

And now allow me to introduce you to . . .

ACT 3: THE SOLUTION

The Presentation is about offering captivating, fulfilling solutions to your prospects in order to secure their devoted business. And that's where applying the Law of the Hook must begin, because even if you've made it this far with a client, a poor presentation can quickly make a prospect disappear. That's why making an early impact is so critical. (Remember the book analogy.) But before we get into the how-tos of Act 3, let's first dispel some of the most common myths about presenting sales solutions.

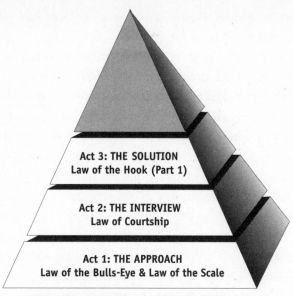

THE HIGH TRUST SALES PYRAMID

SELLING MYTHS TO DISMISS

Since the early twenties, many who have engaged in the training of sales professionals have taught four specific strategies that are supposed to create high-impact sales openings. However, our extensive research over the last two decades no longer supports these claims as effective sales presentation techniques. The truth is that more often than not, practicing the following four questionable techniques will cause your prospects to leave the show before it's over. Before we discuss how to hook your prospect with your sales presentation, let's wipe the slate clean of any misguided selling notions you may have acquired along the way.

Selling Myth #1: Open-ended questions are more effective than closed-ended. Generally speaking, closed-ended questions can be answered with a single yes or no and little explanation, whereas open-ended questions elicit more information from the client. The status quo for years has been that asking questions that let the prospect do the talking is always best. However, this is not the case. The fact is that different sales situations require different types of questions, and to be effective you cannot resolve yourself to one form of questioning.

Remember that your goal is to learn the needs and values that your prospect holds most dear, and this will sometimes require you to be very focused and specific, asking direct questions to ascertain specific answers. And there will be situations that demand you to simply ask and listen. But the point is to not worry about asking the right type of question, and instead focus on getting to truly know the prospect, using whatever questions are most appropriate.

My company's research has shown that, as a general rule, the closer a salesperson gets to closing a deal, the less appropriate open-ended questions become. Think of it this way: If you were spending time with someone with whom you were interested in furthering a relationship, your conversations would not remain on the weather and the last good movie each of you saw. If you were interested in building a long-term relationship with the individual, you'd eventually ask more specific questions that help you get to know the person, not just *about* the person. For example, knowing that an individual is a high school teacher gives you some insight about the person. But knowing that an individual became a high school teacher because he or she is passionate about helping teens discover and develop their gifts helps you know what makes that individual unique; it helps you understand something he or she values in life.

Selling Myth #2: You must demonstrate strong product knowledge. It's good to know all the ins and outs of your product or service, and there is a right time and place to offer that information. But the fact is that if buyers don't trust you or perceive that they stand to receive enough value from a purchase, product knowledge means little. Besides, in most cases premature product pitches lack empathy and are usually interpreted by the buyer as a unilateral tactic. Isn't that what you think when someone does it to you?

As we discussed in the Law of Courtship, it doesn't matter how much you can tell a person about your product or service if you haven't first determined whether your product or service truly meets a real need or fulfills a real value of the prospect. You're just blowing smoke otherwise, and that will quickly turn anyone off.

Selling Myth #3: Features close more sales. Similar to Myth #2, telling a prospect about the "wonderful" features of your product is not an alluring sales technique. The bottom line is that most buyers don't care about features until they know you care about them. Initially, they care about their values, and if you're not speaking on that level, you're communicating on a different wavelength. I'm not telling you to be ignorant of the capabilities and features of your product, but I am telling you that you need to get rid of the notion that people are thrilled to hear about all the "stuff" that your product can do. As we've already said, that stuff doesn't matter if it doesn't in some way touch the prospect's values or needs. Trying to use features to sell your product is usually selfish and rarely successful.

Selling Myth #4: Always be closing. To date, I have personally read or heard over seventy-five different closing techniques. If used today, most would have a negative impact in a selling situation. We have the Alternative of Choice technique, The Hot Potato, Assumptive Close, The Shoe on the Other Foot, The Boomerang, The Take Away, The What Would You Do Now, The Ben Franklin, The Social Proof, The Authoritative, The Bank Account, The Ego Enhancer—and a host of others. You could probably name a few more. And most of the sales training out there suggests that you need to constantly be rotating through these different closing techniques at different stages of the selling process in order to be an effective sales professional—as if your job is to somehow discover which closing technique works by matter of trial and error. I completely disagree with this notion.

For starters, such techniques take your attention off of what prospects are conveying to you—namely their needs and values. Secondly, the closing of a sale, if it's done correctly, should never have to be forced or feel like a roll of the dice. Closing a sale should

> **The truth is that prospects actually close their own sales if you offer valuable solutions to their real needs and values.**

happen naturally because what is offered is highly captivating. Like a great movie, a prospect should be compelled to see the whole thing through. The truth is that prospects actually close their own sales if you offer valuable solutions to their real needs and values. And as you've already learned from the high trust interview in the previous chapter, prospects will tell you the precise benefits they are looking for from your product or service if you take the time to ask them in a professional, strategic manner. That means that when you move to your sales presentation, you can be confident that you're offering your prospects exactly what they've told you they want. That's what the Law of the Hook is all about.

Consider your last car-buying experience. What approach did the salesperson take? Did he sit you down and immediately start spouting knowledge of all the neat gadgets on the inside and outside of the car? Did it impress you? Did it make you want to buy a car from him . . . or just pull off one of his socks and stuff it in his mouth? Did he even ask you what you really wanted? I think most of us have had a car-buying experience like that. Do we go back to that guy for our next car purchase? Do we refer all our friends to that salesperson and that dealership? Most likely not.

But then again, maybe you've had a great experience buying a car. Maybe the salesperson sat you down and asked you what's most important about a car to you? Maybe she shared with you her own frustrations about the car-buying experience and gave you her commitment to doing her best to make your experience enjoyable? Maybe she never even talked about all the gadgets on the car until she had listened to you explain what you wanted in a car. Would you want to buy a car from someone like that? Would you even consider her recommendation for a different car that she thought might be more suitable for your needs? And when you bought a car from her, would you be happy to go back to her again and refer your family and friends to her when they were in the market for a new car? Most likely. And therein lies the beauty of following the Law of the Hook. The power of the early impact often seals the deal.

MAKING AN EARLY IMPACT

We all know that first impressions cannot always be trusted. Haven't you ever met someone and quickly made some conclusions about him that you later found to be completely off base? It happens all the time, doesn't it? At a meeting, a corporate executive meets an executive from a competing firm and immediately assumes he's obtuse and a little suspect of character. After all, he's the enemy. Then, three weeks later, the two cross paths while at a movie with their kids, and they hit it off. They find out that they actually graduated from the same university and their kids currently attend the same elementary school. It changes everything.

Initial perceptions about people are often inaccurate because they are based on shallow knowledge—simply knowing things about a person. And when you consider the stereotype that most associate with salespeople, it becomes increasingly important that you overcome the sleazy, selfish-salesperson stigma as soon as possible. To form an accurate impression of a person, you must go deeper—you must get to know him, his values and desires. That means you must not only get to know your prospects and clients, but you must also allow them to know you as accurately and as early as possible. The best way to do this is by making an early impact that creates a positive and lasting impression.

To ensure that your prospects are hooked and remain hooked for the right reasons, remember the acronym, I.M.P.A.C.T.

Inspirational: If you're not inspired by what you are offering a prospect, then he or she won't be inspired to keep listening to what you have to say. This goes back to the reason you are in sales in the first place. Make a promise to yourself to only sell what you're inspired to sell.

197

Motivational: To create a resounding impact means you must motivate your prospects to act. When a prospect can experience values gratification, the sale is nearly always a done deal.

Professional: It goes without saying that everything about you must be carried out with the utmost professionalism in your sales presentation. That doesn't mean being stuffy or stoic. It simply means that you can't afford to skimp when it comes to dealing with the prospects and clients you desire to serve for life. Think of it this way: If they are the best, they deserve the best.

Applicable: We've already discussed this in great detail, but it bears repeating. Determine beforehand whether the sales effort is truly worth your and your prospect's time, and move forward if and only if the presentation can lead to a long-term, lucrative relationship for both sides.

Considerate: Don't be so revved up to offer your solution that you are inconsiderate to your prospect. Be excited at what you have to offer, but also be willing to listen to what your prospect has to say. Always bear in mind that your most loyal clients will also be your friends and therefore should be treated as such from the very beginning.

Trustworthy: The bottom line is that your offering must be sincere if it is to make a measurable impact. Remember that even if you are a trustworthy person, if your product is not reliable, *you* are not reliable. Make sure that both you and what you sell are aboveboard and worthy to be trusted.

I share the elements of the I.M.P.A.C.T. acronym with you because I want you to fully understand what is behind the scenes of a captivating sales presentation so that when you are ready to offer your prospects attractive solutions to their needs, you do so at the right pace and with the right motives.

OFFERING SIGNIFICANT SOLUTIONS

Act 3 is one of the shortest components of the High Trust Selling System but it's the most critical for creating a lasting IMPACT. That's because it's during your initial sales presentation that you finally get to shine. In fact, if you've done the preliminary work of ascertaining your prospects' values and needs, and you are confident that your product or service can fulfill them, your sales presentation should be like offering a well-thought-out gift to a friend. And like choosing the perfect giftwrap, you must ensure that the words you choose enhance your prospects' enthusiasm to receive the gift.

One of the greatest pieces of advice I ever received was very early in my career. One of my first mentors told me that I should never have to wing it when it came to presenting something that would make the sale. It was soon after receiving that advice that I took one of my greatest professional strides. I began to take the needs that my prospects shared with me during high trust interviews and created scripts for how my product or relationship could address them. I also began compiling the needs, figuring that many of them would be similar. I jotted them down in my "Success Journal" along with the scripts that I had written to address them. I then recorded the scripts on tape, ten times each, and listened to the tape until I could recite them professionally and naturally.

Please understand that knowing my scripts word for word was never my goal, and that wouldn't have been the right goal anyway. When it comes to sales presentation success, memorization is not the key: knowing what to say is—and that's what Act 3 is all about.

In order to present well, you have to be thinking like your clients ahead of time. You have to put yourself in their shoes and determine what you would ask and desire in the same situation. When you understand your prospects' greatest needs and values, you can design an educated script that allows you to prepare to address them naturally, professionally, and confidently. That way, when you conduct a sales presentation, you aren't fumbling with words or making offers that aren't valid. Let me give you an example of how this worked for me when I was new to sales.

At the age of twenty-two, I was terrified to start my first sales job. All I didn't need (but often got) was a prospect telling me she wanted to work with someone with a lot of experience. I didn't have any. But I knew that if I was going to have an impact I would somehow need to be able to address this need that my prospects were conveying to me. I knew I needed to be prepared to solve the need before the next time it was expressed. As a result, I sat down and within an hour had the following script practiced and ready to go:

> "While I might be new to the mortgage business, I am not new to the idea of taking great care of my customers. In fact, for the last six years, I have been instrumental in helping a multistore sporting-goods chain build the systems that enable them to take great care of their customers. The reason I chose ABC Financial as my employer is that they've been in the mortgage business for over ten years, have helped over fifty thousand families successfully buy homes, and are committed to the same level of customer service that I am. And I believe that their experience combined with my own will ultimately produce the results you desire."

I never had to waffle on that need again. In fact, within about two months, I had recorded over thirty additional needs that my prospects had expressed to me, with solution scripts to address each of them. As a result, my sales soared and I remained one of the top producers in my company every month from that point forward. I know you can do the same thing. Start keeping track of every need your prospects (and existing clients) express to you. Write every one of them down; then create a script that conveys how you will address and solve those needs. (Note that integrity is important here—don't write a script that expresses something you cannot or will not do). If you were to create one new script a week and practice it until your delivery was natural, I am certain you would elevate to the next level of sales success.

As a quick reminder, here are some of the most common needs that you are likely to hear prospects say they have of you. While I share these with you so that you have a clear picture of what we're talking about, don't limit your prospects to these needs. Just listen to what they tell you in the high trust interview and apply those to the scripts you create.

> experience
> knowledge
> integrity
> professionalism
> communication
> accessibility
> flexibility
> responsiveness
> creativity
> availability
> reliability

And, once again, here are the most common needs your prospects are likely to say they have of your product, service, or company:

> location
> delivery and turnaround
> product/technical support
> reputation
> innovation
> financial strength
> market share
> product line
> R & D (research & development)
> guarantees

Regardless of what needs and values your prospects express, *the key to Act 3 is preparing solutions before presenting solutions.* That's what it takes to make a significant impact right away. And while it may take an extra commitment of time on the front end, once you gain confidence in performing Act 3, it will pay huge dividends.

Act 4: The Action

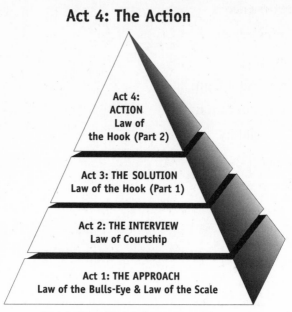

THE HIGH TRUST SALES PYRAMID

The most exciting part of any sales presentation is hearing prospects say yes after you've asked for their business. Once you've made an impact with your presentation, there will come a point when you must ask for the prospect's business. If you've done everything right to this point of the sales interaction, Act 4 should be easy. In fact, there will even be occasions when you don't even have to ask for business, but only confirm what a prospect has already made known to you.

For instance, let's say you are a contractor selling home remodeling services and a potential client—a middle-aged couple wanting to finish their basement—asks you to come and give a bid on the work. Since the couple only knows of you from some former neighbors, and you know very little of them, you might begin an informal High Trust Interview while you walk with them through their home. If they tell you that the basement is for their son who is graduating from college soon, you know family is very important to them. If they then tell you that he will graduate in four months, you know that utmost efficiency is also very important for this particular sale. You might continue your informal interview by asking about their long-term plans for the home, or even about their retirement plans. Then you'd obviously discuss their desires for the details of the basement itself, which may include asking what types of interests and hobbies their son has, or even his plans for work—all of which would help you learn not only about the individuals but also give you the means to customize your service to perfectly fit their and their son's desires and needs. Throughout this process, you will not only have built trust with the potential client, you will have gained the resources to make an effective, captivating presentation that has a high likelihood of being well-received—quite possibly without you even asking for the business.

The following is a very simple, four-step process for actively shifting top prospects to trusting partners by keeping them captivated.

Step 1: Know when to ask. Only at the end of a sales presentation, when you have thoroughly completed Acts 1 through 3 of the HTSS, should you even think about asking for business. In rare cases, a prospect may move you to Act 4 much quicker than normal, but usually that's because a level of trust already existed in your relationship. In typical scenarios, when you've taken a prospect from the approach to the interview to the presentation, and all signs are still go, all that's left for you to do is determine the appropriate time to ask. Remember, you can have confidence that, more often than not, your prospect will be ready to buy if you've come this far. Nonetheless, I've found that knowing how to read a prospect's buying signals helps to avoid an awkward situation. Here are a few to look and listen for:

A. Positive body language

> *Leaning forward, smiling, nodding the head, becoming more active in the conversation.*

B. Price interest: the prospect asking,

> ➤ *"How much does it cost?"*
> ➤ *"What is the price of this one?"*
> ➤ *"Is that all it costs?"*

C. Value Interest: the prospect asking,

> ➤ *"You would do that for me?"*
> ➤ *"It can do all of that?"*
> ➤ *"It comes with all of that?"*

D. Questions about deliverables: the prospect asking,

> ➤ *"How soon can I have it?"*
> ➤ *"When could it be delivered?"*
> ➤ *"Could I have it by then?"*
> ➤ *"Could you do it by then?"*

E. Request for referrals: the prospect asking,

> ➤ *"Who else is using this that I know?"*
> ➤ *"Do you have a list of clients whom you've served?"*

F. Positive comments

> ➤ *"That sounds like what I have been looking for."*
> ➤ *"I love the way this feels."*
> ➤ *"This is top-quality stuff."*
> ➤ *"I can't believe after all these years that I don't have one of these."*

There are many more signals that will help you indicate when a prospect is likely to buy, but the key to receiving a positive response is to have done the legwork up front.

In our illustration, the couple's positive reaction to your needs-specific solutions for customizing their basement would indicate that they are ready to move forward. Or they may ask something less subtle, like, "When could you start your work?" Either way, the couple's positive reactions to your needs-specific suggestions—before a bid is even made on the job—would be a green light indicator that they are willing to move forward.

In the end, Act 4 should seem like the natural progression of your relationship, the imminent result of all you've done thus far. Trust me, when you are careful to follow the HTSS, and your audience is captivated, you will begin to look forward to asking for business.

Step 2: Know how to ask. When you're ready to ask for business, you would say something like, "Mr. and Mrs. Smith, based on what I have proposed [what you've seen, how you feel, your evident interest], do you feel we have a basis for doing business together?" This is the only closing question you need if you have done everything right to this point, if you've established a level of trust. Nothing fancy, not seventy-five different closing techniques to memorize. One simple, straightforward question that elicits one of two answers: yes or no. If a prospect's answer is yes, your high trust relationship is off and running. But don't forget—even if prospects answer no at this point and you're confident they are the type of clients you desire, you can still turn things around. We'll discuss this in a minute. First let's finish out the steps that follow when a prospect says yes.

Step 3: Know what to say next. It's important to maintain the momentum of the relationship by agreeing on what the next step is. I always advise my students to try to avoid turning this part over to the prospect. I am a big believer that you must maintain control from this point to the end by keeping the dialogue alive. One of the most effective ways to do so is by reoffering your Unique Value Proposition that you originally offered in your Approach. Remember, if you resolve to give, you will receive.

For the couple in our illustration that might mean reiterating the original desires that they told you they wanted for the basement and for their son. Touching on this again will help remind them that your focus is first on their needs and values.

Step 4: Know what to do next. Every new client relationship must have an active growth plan if it's to flourish from the start. Regular partnership planning keeps the energy alive in a high trust relationship and fosters clients' desire to continue giving you their business. I'll go deep on this in the final chapters, but for now understand that it's most effective to set up a series of contacts up front so that you can focus and grow the relationship early on.

In our illustration, that would mean sitting down with the couple and determining a remodeling schedule that they are comfortable with and that is feasible to you, the contractor. From there you would set up not only a series of 2 or 3 progress meetings during the remodeling process, you would also indicate your desire to continue a mutually beneficial relationship with the couple and their friends and family in the coming years after the basement is finished.

THE INTERMISSION

We would all like to be in a position where we don't get objections. But no matter what you do, people will always fear change and will often find some reason to object—even if it's just out of habit. That said, however, the number-one reason salespeople get objections is because they haven't effectively followed the selling process you've learned in this book. In other words, objections are mostly the fault of the seller.

Objections are the symptoms of a poor selling process.

If you do too much talking during a presentation and throw lots of features their way, it increases prospects' sensitivity to price. If you talk too much about unrelated benefits, it increases prospects' sensitivity to integrity. If you don't thoroughly present solutions, it increases prospects' concern for capacity or capability. What I'm getting at is that objections are the symptoms of a poor selling process, which in the end merely propagates a lack of trust. But if you master the process of approaching, interviewing, presenting, and asking for business, you will reduce your objections significantly, if not eliminate them all together.

Nonetheless, if you understand how to address and offer a solution for a need that arises from a high trust interview, you can effectively address objections the same way when they do arise. By taking time to ascertain the root of an objection—by asking simple questions like you did in your interview—you can determine whether it's connected to a real need that you can solve. Once you've managed objections a few times you will find that most are directly connected to prospects' needs and can be solved by preparing simple scripts (which you may have already written and practiced). Before long, most of your objection management duties will simply become objection prevention—an intermission in your sales performance, but certainly not the conclusion.

There will be an occasion, however, when a bull's-eye prospect will say no to your solution offering, despite effective preparation, presentation, and objection management. At this point, it's important to remember that if you thought enough of the prospect to target him in the first place, you should not give up immediately. While it's important that you don't spend an unreasonable amount of time fostering relationships with prospects that have yet to provide business, it is certainly reasonable to maintain regular contact with such prospects in hopes of eventually securing high trust and, subsequently, their business. I didn't know it at the time, but this is precisely what I did when I sent my prospect a series of value-adding messages each month over an eighteen-month period of time before I got my first sale from her. (You'll recall I shared this story in Chapter 9.)

When it comes to maintaining contact with top prospects that are not ready to do business, I recommend that you keep two things in mind. First, make certain that time committed to investing in the prospect wouldn't be better spent on deepening relationships with existing high trust clients. Then, once that has been established, commit to adding value to the prospect through letters, phone calls, E-mails, etc., once a month for a minimum of two years. While some prospects will commit their business to you in less time, many of the top prospects in your field will have an established relationship with a competitor; and that usually takes more time to overcome.

Consider two salespeople, we'll call them Susan and Brian, who work for the same company. Both prospect and sell from the same number of pre-established leads every week, and both have the same resources at their disposal in terms of marketing and follow-up material. However, Susan makes three times as much as Brian does— and that has been the case for the last three years. Why? For one main reason.

When Brian receives an objection from a prospect, he takes it personally and lets the relationship go. As he sees it, his job is to find those prospects that will meet *his* needs—who will find nothing objectionable about him, his selling techniques, or his product. And that's why Brian doesn't do much selling—or rather, why Brian's prospects don't do much buying, at least from him.

Susan, on the other hand, goes about things differently. When she receives an objection from a potential client, she sees it as an opportunity to improve, an opportunity to better customize her offering and thus more thoroughly meet the potential clients' needs and secure their business. In fact, many of her stable clients today—ten of them to be exact—are actually former prospects of Brian's who had objections that he was unwilling to manage. Not only do those clients provide her business that keeps her well ahead of her colleague, they also make up nearly half of her entire client base from which she generates three times as much sales and income as Brian—and she spends half as much time in the office.

Remember that the goal of all objection management is to foster a deeper level of trust and maintain the captivation of your audience. In most cases, you will not have a difficult time accomplishing this if you've been careful to follow the High Trust Selling System. Ultimately, if your audience is truly captivated—whether immediately following your solution offering or after some effective objection management and follow up—they will want to stay with you to the end. And in the elite echelon of high trust selling that means your business will realize the full value of their relationships. That is the ultimate goal of every sales relationship.

That brings us to the subject of the next chapter: the Law of Incubation, which says that the most profitable relationships mature over time.

SALES LEADERSHIP APPLICATION

Ensuring that your sales team understands and applies the Law of the Hook might require some vulnerability and humility on your part. Teaching the Law could require you to unteach some ineffective methods that have been passed down through your company's hierarchy. But if your goal is to take your success and that of your sales team to the highest level, you must be willing to give up to go up. I encourage you to take the steps necessary to fully implement the High Trust Selling System as a part of your teams' regular training so that it eventually becomes the standard by which your company does sales. While it may take some time and some additional effort on your part to get started, trust me when I say that it will be well worth it in the end.

CHAPTER THIRTEEN

The Law of Incubation

The Most Profitable Relationships
Mature over Time

R ecently my company secured one of the most lucrative relationships in our history—a seven-figure, multiyear deal. But we had been adding value to the former bull's-eye prospect for over three years, first establishing high trust then fostering that trust until the relationship matured into a long-term partnership. And that's where the real profits loomed. But the truth is that we're still not done adding value. As long as we are in business together, my company will continually seek to meet the maturing expectations of our partner, as they will seek to meet ours, because we know that's the only way to realize the full value of the partnership.

When a business relationship is a right match, as it grows so does its earning potential. A friend and client, Jeff Lake, exemplifies this approach to maximizing client relationships.

By his own admission, for years Jeff was an eight-ounce bottle with sixteen ounces of fluid in it. He was working seventy hours a week and spending 75 percent of that time prospecting and attempting to build new relationships and only 25 percent of his time fostering existing relationships with paying clients. And while he had gotten pretty good at keeping all his plates spinning—doing just enough to keep most everyone happy—his quality of life had gone downhill. He and his wife had just welcomed a baby girl into the world that year, and his ever-increasing time at the office was sapping time from his family. Not only that, he wasn't even close to realizing the full value that each of his existing clients could bring him. Cognitively, he knew something needed to give; but practically speaking, he wasn't sure what to do. He tried this and that for a few years but nothing seemed to stick. He was still working long hours and found himself more and more disturbed at his lack of quality time to do what really mattered, especially off the job. The thought that stuck in his mind most was coming home one day to a little girl who hardly knew her daddy. That, he determined, wasn't going to happen.

In 1993, Jeff decided to do some research outside his industry to determine how other sales professionals maintained a high level of success while keeping their quality of life intact. He was doing well, producing about $60 million a year in sales, but he was determined to find a way to reclaim a high quality of life and still maintain his productivity.

As a result of his research, some coaching, and a few seminars, Jeff realized that what he needed to do was change his approach to client relationships. He was spending too much time trying to build new relationships and not spending enough time fostering his existing client relationships to realize their maximum value. While he knew it would take some time and quite possibly a drop in profit, Jeff was committed to making this change. Part of this process was scaling back on the number of clients he worked with in order to completely serve those whom he deemed the cream of the crop. He began meeting with his clients and explaining this change in approach, and an overwhelming majority applauded his efforts. They, too, felt that quality of life was more important than anything.

Since 1993, Jeff has remained committed to his strategy of realizing the full value of each client relationship. In fact, he now spends just 25 percent of his time looking for new business—75 percent of his time is spent building and growing his existing relationships to maturity. And while his profits did drop slightly at first, he and his team of four now produce $250 million a year in sales—a 400 percent increase. And most importantly, he only works an average of forty-five hours a week and takes ten weeks of vacation a year with his growing family.

To understand the Law of Incubation as Jeff does, you have to recognize one thing: There are no shortcuts to building the most lucrative, long-lasting relationships. Don't get me wrong here. Following the HTSS will certainly secure most of the high trust relationships you desire—and those relationships will dramatically increase your profits in the first few years. But to maximize your profits over time, you must understand the way relationships work.

Go back to our dating analogy. How many stories have you heard of men who invested a lot of time, energy, and creativity trying to captivate a beautiful woman in order to win a date with her? Those stories are fairly common, right? (And so are sales appointments.) Maybe you've experienced a similar story. But if you asked the guy pursuing the woman if he thought he'd reached his goal by landing one date, he'd be quick to correct you. Getting her to say yes to a date is just the first step—albeit an important step—if the ultimate goal is a lasting marriage. Beyond that first date, important steps must be taken to grow the dating relationship, steps that will determine whether the two will get married (Law of Courtship). Furthermore, once the two are married, that's really just the beginning of their life together. Beyond the marriage vows the couple must come to terms with all that is necessary to ensure the marriage's success. And in the end, the man who wins the woman's heart for good—and vice versa—is the one whose actions have consistently fostered the trust that was established on those first few dates. Something very similar must happen if you desire your sales relationships to reach their potential.

A LESSON YOU SHOULD ONLY LEARN ONCE!

Ninety-five percent of salespeople go 95 percent of the way and get only 5 percent of what's available to them. Five percent of salespeople go 100 percent of the way and get 95 percent of what's available to them. You must decide in which group you want to be.

The Law of Incubation says that the most profitable relationships mature over time. To be certain that you get this before we go any further, I want you to understand that we're not talking about merely having tenacity and a never-give-up attitude. Those are certainly admirable qualities, but they're not nearly enough to make a relationship last. Relationships that are fruitful and enduring are not comprised of parties that are committed to perseverance. (If that were all it took for a relationship to last, the national divorce rate wouldn't be nearly sixty percent.) The most productive relationships are comprised of people who are committed to consistently adding value where value is most needed. Incubation is the process by which you consistently add value to a client for as long as you do business together, knowing that over time that will ensure that the relationship matures to fruition. Think about it this way: A girl doesn't stay with a guy because she's overwhelmed by his persistence. She stays with him because of the value that he adds to her life, and the value that she adds to his.

RELATIONSHIPS THAT REACH MATURITY

The salesperson who adds value after the sale clearly demonstrates that the relationship is more important than revenue, and the person is more important than profits. Incubation is not about getting a sales relationship going. That's what the High Trust Selling System is for. Incubation is about keeping a sales relationship flowing. While adding value is critical throughout the selling process, following the Law of Incubation is about using the long-term transference of value as your main client-retention tool.

> **The salesperson who adds value after the sale clearly demonstrates that the relationship is more important than revenue, and the person is more important than profits.**

Salespeople are notorious for landing a sale and then never doing anything beyond that to sustain the relationship. Most give their one-time clients no reason to continue in a relationship with them, and they are therefore constantly stuck in an acquisition mode where the stress is high and the stakes are never certain. The truth is that many salespeople can "get" a sale if they want it bad enough. That's not to say that they are getting the sale the right way—it is to say that if salespeople make enough calls, bang on enough doors, and do a good enough job of begging that some poor soul will eventually feel sorry for them and give them business. It's no wonder so many salespeople hate their jobs.

I don't tell you all that to depress you, but rather to show you that often the main difference between the mediocre salesperson and the high trust sales professional is how they treat their clients after a sale. The mediocre salesperson immediately moves on to the next victim after a sale, leaving the relationship with his last client to wither and eventually die. On the other hand, high trust salespeople know that the most profitable relationships are a result of a time-honored investment, and they therefore take the steps necessary to retain their best clients for as long as possible—the longer the relationship, the more lucrative it can be. And you must do the same if you desire to reach your potential.

To be successful in high trust selling you must always have a balance of prospects who are being converted to first-time clients and first-time clients who are being converted to lifetime clients. And while the percentage of time that you spend on securing new clients will probably decrease as your relationships with existing clients mature, the Law of Incubation ensures that every client with whom you do business becomes and remains a client for life.

The most obvious long-term impact of the incubation strategy is client profitability—getting the most business possible from those with whom you do business. The less obvious—but equally significant—long-term benefit of incubation has to do with long-term client referrals. A relationship founded on mutual trust that is fostered over time through a consistent value-adding strategy is the most profitable kind of relationship that a sales professional can ever have. And besides, why would you want to invest in a relationship and not reap the full benefit? Once you've done the leg-work up front to determine that the relationship is worth the effort, it makes sense to see it through to complete maturity. To not do so is the equivalent of pursuing, dating, and courting a person only to call the relationship off the day before the wedding. And no one wants the effects of that.

SECURING YOUR FAIR SHARE

Often, salespeople measure their success through the market share numbers that their companies post. And while I think market share is an important gauge of a company's success, "client share" is the truest measure of a salesperson's relationship success.

The easiest way to understand the client share concept is to think of market share as a horizontal concept and client share as a vertical concept.

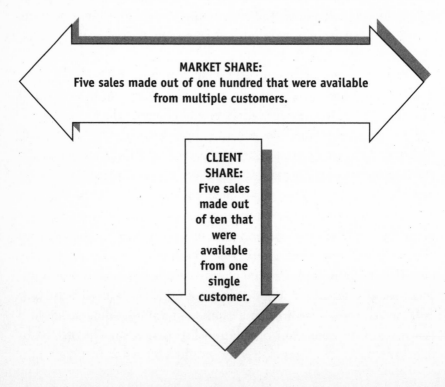

MARKET SHARE:
Five sales made out of one hundred that were available
from multiple customers.

CLIENT
SHARE:
Five sales
made out
of ten that
were
available
from one
single
customer.

Let's say that over the course of a month, there are one hundred sales in your given territory that are available to you and your competitors. If you landed five of those available sales then you'd end up with a 5 percent market share for the month. Generally speaking, to maximize your market share you must sell as much of your product to as many clients as you possibly can. In essence, you must spread yourself out as wide as possible—the greater the number of clients, the greater the number of sales. And after all is said and done, if you ended up averaging a 7 percent market share per month, you'd probably be doing pretty well in most sales markets. But the problem is that usually means spending a lot less time with a lot more people. In effect, to increase your market share numbers you generally have to spread yourself thinner, which results in shallower, untapped relationships and a very unstable business foundation.

On the other hand, if you were striving to increase your client share, you would focus on fostering deeper relationships with fewer people—spreading yourself thicker, so to speak. Using the example as above: If in the same thirty days you focused on only one client who offered the potential of ten sales (directly through the client herself or indirectly through her referrals), and you secured half of them, you would end up with a 50 percent client share. And here's the beauty in this strategy: While you still end up with the same net amount of sales (five), there is much more room to improve, because working with only one client takes much less time and effort. In fact, your average client share can actually decrease while your revenues increase. Here's how.

Let's say that in the next month you managed to finish with a 60 percent client share with your original client but only managed a 30 percent client share with another client whom you took on, closing only three of the ten potential sales that client offered. While your average client share for the month decreased to 45 percent, you still managed to close a total of nine sales, nearly doubling your production from the month before. I don't know about you, but spending less time on fewer clients to make more money sounds much better than pounding the pavement or the phone pad unendingly for the purpose of dealing with more and more clients who don't know me from Adam. I have a sense you feel the same way.

Focusing on client share is about increasing the potential of each sales relationship without increasing your time on the job. Essentially, the difference between a market-share mentality and a client-share strategy is the difference between shooting a shotgun and shooting an arrow. The first tends to be messy with low accuracy; the second is efficient with acute accuracy. The truth of the matter is that if you are careful to put the Law of Incubation into practice regularly, fostering the bull's-eye relationships you've established using the HTSS, you will find that selling doesn't have to be stressful at all and can actually be very fulfilling on a daily basis, because in the end it's all about initiating and preserving loyal relationships.

LOWER COSTS, HIGHER POTENTIAL

To follow the Law of Incubation you must strive to increase client share instead of market share. It all comes down to acquisition costs versus retention costs.

Generally, market share increases by acquisition. The more clients you acquire in your given territory, the greater your market share. On the other hand, client share mainly increases by retention. The greater your client retention the greater your number of sales from each client, and hence the greater your client share. Now consider the costs of acquisition versus retention. Which would you say costs more in terms of effort, time, and money: to secure a new sale from a new client or secure a repeat sale from an existing client? Obviously, getting repeat sales costs much less, because the acquisition costs no longer exist. On the other hand, continually landing new sales from new clients means continually taking on more acquisition costs, which research shows are about five to seven times higher than retention costs. Put it this way: When you focus on increasing client share (retention), your costs always decrease the longer each client remains. And if you stay with this strategy, you will ultimately get to the place where your acquisition costs are at a minimum because the majority of your business flows from those clients whom you've retained through high trust relationships.

REAPING YOUR HARVEST

Shallow relationships or deep relationships? It's your call. If you go shallow, you will constantly be digging and planting to keep your sales career alive. This means a constant infusion of new prospects will be the absolute requirement for you to continue to survive in the sales profession. That's hard work. But if you go deep with your best relationships, planting then growing trust one client at a time, you will not have to plant very often. Rather, like a dependable harvest, you will spend your time reaping the fruits of your labor through repeat business and expanded referrals.

In charting the courses of thousands of sales students over the years, one thing I've found that acts as a significant catalyst for making a commitment to following the Law of Incubation is determining the lifetime monetary value of clients. Understanding the long-term value that a client can add to your business usually impacts most salespeople dramatically because they can tangibly see the huge rewards that lie in store if the relationship matures.

Following are several examples of the long-term value that a client can bring to a sales business (including my company) that will show the significance of applying the Law of Incubation.

The Duncan Group Client Value Model (Products)

A. The average transaction amount	$250
B. Number of sales per year	2
C. Revenue per year (A x B)	$500
D. Client Life Cycle	5 years
E. Client Cycle Value	$2,500

Indirect/Word-of-mouth value

F. High trust client tells ten others. (E x 10)	$25,000
G. Referral Revenue @ 25 percent	$6,250
Total Lifetime Value of a Client (G+E)	**$8,750**

The Office Computer Supplier

A. The average transaction amount	$3,500
B. Number of sales per year	5
C. Revenue per year (A x B)	$17,500
D. Client Life Cycle	5 years
E. Client Cycle Value	$87,500

Indirect/Word-of-mouth value

F. High trust client tells ten others. (E x 10)	$875,000
G. Referral Revenue @ 25 percent	$218,750
Total Lifetime Value of a Client (G+E)	**$306,250**

The Mercedes Benz Dealership

A. The average transaction amount	$70,000
B. Number of sales every three years per buyer	1/3
C. Revenue per year (A x B)	$23,300
D. Client Life Cycle	20 years
E. Client Cycle Value	$466,000

Indirect/Word-of-mouth value

F. High trust client tells ten others. (E x 10)	$4,660,000
G. Referral Revenue @ 25 percent	$1,165,000
Total Lifetime Value of a Client (G+E)	**$1,631,000**

As you can see, once you know how much a high trust relationship is worth to you and your company, you'll want to retain it as long as you can. When you take a look at the Lifetime Value Models above, it's easy to see that there is substantial value in long-term client retention. It increases profitability, fosters loyalty, expands referrals, and secures cash flow. In short, it's the first step to securing the most out of every sales relationship. And generally speaking, when it comes to retaining the best clients, you need to remember one simple truth: You must do more to keep a client than you did to get the client. That doesn't mean you have to continually win a client's trust over and over. It simply means that high trust relationships must be continuously nurtured if they are to reap a full harvest. As in any relationship, once trust is earned, it is then matured over time though consistency and integrity.

You must do more to keep a client than you did to get the client.

In short, to best retain the high trust clients you have acquired, you must move the relationship over time from a professional level to a partnership level. I'm not telling you to sacrifice your level of professionalism and take on some sort of buddy-buddy, sit-on-the-couch-and-eat-chips-together mentality. I am saying that for your high trust relationships to mature you must move them beyond the boundaries of the seller/buyer affiliation to a place of partnership governed by give-and-take.

It's simple: If you want to maximize the relationships you've formed, you cannot be the only one giving. While you will always continue to add value to your high trust clients, your relationships will not reach their potential until your clients also give back to you in the form of both repeat and referral business. That's the culmination of following the Law of Incubation. However, as you most certainly know from your nonsales relationships, give-and-take never happens accidentally. Your clients' motivation to give you more business and to stay connected to you is largely a function of your initiation and leadership. In other words, you must be strategic about both forming and fostering productive partnerships.

Essentially, forming a strategic partnership is purposefully seeking agreeable terms for a mutually beneficial relationship. And that's what you must do with each of your newly acquired high trust clients if you desire to reach your potential. Two of my clients, Tim Braheem and Terry Moerler, understand this very well.

Tim knew about Terry for some time before the two became partners. Terry had a wonderful reputation for being one of the best sales professionals in her industry. And as Tim saw it first, there was tremendous potential for both of them to increase their profits dramatically if a strategic relationship was formed. There was only one problem: Terry had a seven-year relationship with another salesperson in Tim's industry and was very loyal to that individual—something Tim respected very much. She referred business to that salesperson and received business back. It seemed to be working well; nevertheless, Tim waited for the right opportunity to meet Terry. He knew that any long-term business relationship with her would have to start with a friendship built on trust. And before long, an opportunity arose to meet her.

In that first meeting between the two, Tim did nothing but get to know Terry—something that made a lasting impression on her. The meeting that was supposed to be less than an hour lasted nearly two hours and was focused entirely on conveying ideas and building a friendship—but not on getting business from each other. That would come later. For several months, the two continued to meet on a regular basis to catch up and bounce ideas off each other that they could apply to their existing relationships in their respective industries. During this time, Tim was fostering the relationship to maturity, which he knew would take some time. Then, after several months of meeting, one day it happened. Terry had become increasingly dissatisfied with the partner she had been using in Tim's industry, and she brought up the idea of forming a new strategic partnership with him. Of course, Tim was already prepared for this, so he shared with her his thoughts on the matter. And that day Tim and Terry took their trust relationship to the next level.

Today, Tim and Terry's relationship is still maturing. The two still meet once a month for two hours to make sure they are doing everything they can to meet each other's needs and maximize the value of the relationship. And even though the relationship has yet to realize its full potential, it certainly has produced much fruit over the last few years. In fact, last year Terry referred Tim over $18 million in sales. And this year, Tim's referrals alone will make Terry over $100,000 in income. That's the kind of valuable relationship that results from following the Law of Incubation.

For your clients to become partners and remain your partners for good, you must continually share a vested interest in each other's success—like Tim and Terry do. In fact, there are four steps that you should take in order to consistently add value to your clients and maximize the potential of your relationships. As you consider each of these steps, understand that once this system is in place, it is meant to be sustained throughout your sales career.

Incubation Step 1: Develop a three-tier ranking of your clients. Clearly, for Tim and Terry, they ranked at the top of each other's client list. Terry referred Tim as much or more than any of his other partners, and Tim did the same for Terry. Which clients are your most valuable? Which produce the highest percentage of sales? Which are more likely to refer you more business? Which clients have the most potential to you and your firm? When you answer these questions you can establish your ranking system. (Remember from the Law of the Hourglass that the smallest population of your clients probably produces the greatest revenue for your business).

Here's an example:

Client Ranking	# of Clients	% of Sales
Level One: VIP	5	60
Level Two: Premier	60	25
Level Three: Standard	35	15

Incubation Step 2: Commit to a specific investment for each prospect and/or client. For example, if I know that a loyal client for our firm is worth $500 dollars a year, then I need to answer the question: "How much do we want to regularly invest in that client to ensure high loyalty?" I generally tell students that they should come up with three investment levels. For example, for Level One clients (those with whom you have established a high trust relationship and who can be the most profitable), invest 15 percent of their value back into them. For Level Two clients (those with whom you've just begun to do business), invest 10 percent of their value back into them. And for Level Three clients (those with whom you intend to do business at some point in the future), invest 5 percent back into them. Ultimately, you decide the amounts you will invest back into clients to retain them, but there is no magic to it. Like any investment, you want to measure your return. Simply invest more where there is more high trust and more potential for business. That's why Tim and Terry continue to invest in each other. Invest the least where clients' value and trust are not yet established. Note that this step also applies to your investment of time.

Incubation Step 3: For each tier, decide your annual contact plan. For Tim and Terry this means meeting formally at least 12 times a year. Like them, you should have an annual contact management plan for each one of your clients. At the end of this chapter, I will show you how to use contact management to master the follow-up procedure with each client. Here however, you need to simply understand that you must plan to have more contact with your best customers than you will with your marginal customers. Here is a sample of a pace of contact over the course of a year for three sample groups.

CLIENT CONTACT PLAN

Level One: VIP clients receive thirteen contacts per year.
Level Two: Premier clients receive nine contacts per year.
Level Three: Standard clients receive five contacts per year.

These points of contact do not include necessary calls or meetings that must be made to discuss or generate sales. They are strictly to create loyalty and build trust.

The goal of Step 3 is to structure relationships with VIP clients, grow relationships with Premier clients, and maintain relationships with Standard clients/prospects that offer future potential.

Incubation Step 4: Collaborate regularly. The greatest advantage you have over your competition is knowing your clients better than they do. While you don't need to constantly revisit the high trust interview process (from the Law of Courtship), you must get in the habit of continually interviewing your clients through weekly or monthly partnership planning sessions in which you both ascertain existing needs and seek to discover new needs; and also through annual client reviews in which you both revisit your progress for the previous year and determine if there are any ways to improve the productivity of the relationship. Along with their formal meetings every month, Tim and Terry talk on the phone several times a week in order to both exchange business and ensure top-quality service to each other's clients.

> As in any relationship, the better in tune you are with your
> partner's needs, the more easily you can
> meet that person's needs.

There are no perfect formulas for employing an ongoing-needs discovery routine with your clients. The goal is simple: As in any relationship, the better in tune you are with your partner's needs, the more easily you can meet that person's needs.

This type of partnership strategy continually boosts your relationships forward and ensures that your first order from a client is not the only order you take. It helps you remain in touch with your clients in order to avoid any gaps in meeting their needs. It also helps you know what to expect from your clients in terms of repeat and referral business. If you recall, in Chapter 10 (the Law of the Scale) I shared with you about a client named Tim Broadhurst whose $80 million a year in sales comes from the repeat and referral business of only twelve clients. (Not to mention that it affords him and his family the luxury of about three months of vacation a year!) His results are a function of his keen ability to continually foster his key high trust relationships, adding value to his partners and thus maximizing the potential they add to his business. And the same can be true of you if you are careful to follow the Law of Incubation in your business.

IF YOU FOLLOW UP WITH THEM, THEY WILL FOLLOW THROUGH WITH YOU

There is no greater discipline in the high trust selling process than adding value. A regular dose of value decreases the likelihood that your clients will be wooed by your competitors, and therefore increases the stability of your business. In fact, when you consistently add significant value to your clients over time, they will eventually come to a point at which they cannot imagine doing business with, or referring business to, anyone else. That's when you know you've secured a profitable, productive client-for-life.

The truth is that, from beginning to end, the high trust selling process is about adding value to take the relationship to the next level, and the next, and so on. Take a look at how it works:

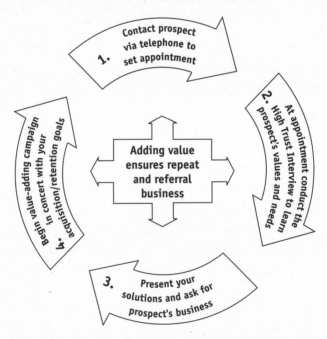

The fundamental application of the Law of Incubation is following up with every prospect and client you want to retain for life so that they follow through with repeat and referral business for you, for life. This cycle begins when you start practicing the High Trust Selling System and continues as long as you are a sales professional, whether you are acquiring or retaining high trust clients. Ultimately, consistent, value-adding follow-up with both your prospects and clients will set you apart from the majority of all salespeople.

Creating Customer Loyalty

By now you should know that the key to selling success is building loyal, lucrative relationships by consistently learning and satisfying the needs of your clients. And the better you know your clients the more you can satisfy their needs and create more loyalty. But I want you to be clear on something: The only thing that guarantees client loyalty is high trust cultivated by consistent, value-rich follow-up.

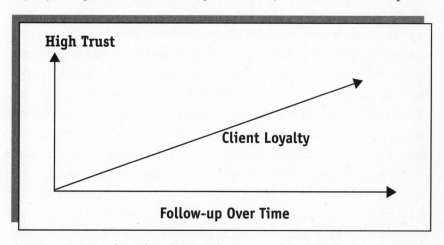

As you can see, client loyalty is a function of both high trust and follow-up over time. High trust by itself will raise the probability of client loyalty in your business, but without actions to back it up, its potential will never be tapped. This is what happens so often when salespeople do a great job of establishing trust with a client for one sale, but have trouble securing a second sale with the same client because they did nothing to validate the client's trust between sales. You can't have loyalty without high trust; and trusting clients will not remain loyal unless you have follow-up systems. If you're going to spend the time finding prospects and converting them to high trust clients, I'm sure you want to keep them. This is accomplished through the daily discipline of contact management.

You can't have loyalty without high trust; and trusting clients will not remain loyal unless you have follow-up systems.

STAYING IN CLOSE CONTACT

The simple truth is that you can't add value efficiently today without maintaining an accurate bank of information on your clients. Getting this information, using it respectfully, and keeping it updated is necessary for staying in close enough contact with your high trust clients to consistently add value to their lives.

In the grand scheme of high trust selling, the role of a contact management system is to effectively record and efficiently utilize client information for the purpose of increasing and securing client loyalty—such information as the name of the person who originally referred the client to you, the client's core values, his or her most important needs, buying strategy, expectation for the relationship, birthday and that of his or her immediate family members, anniversary if the client is married, and any other pertinent information that you would consider helpful for meeting your client's needs and maintaining a fruitful relationship. Consider your client data as a long-term economic asset that must be managed well in the short term. The more you know about your clients—what they need and want, and how to most efficiently meet those desires—the more valuable that asset becomes and the easier it will be for you to maximize the earning potential of each relationship.

In the end, however, it's not the sophistication of your contact management system that will determine if you've built a high trust sales business. It's what you do with the information that you've gained. It's whether you consistently and relevantly add value to you best clients over time. Remember that adding value is the only way to secure long-term loyalty and trust. The more you do, the more business you will get.

That's why, in the end, it's all about service.

SALES LEADERSHIP APPLICATION

As the leader, have you given your salespeople the idea that they can achieve lasting success overnight? If you have, it may be time to eat your words. While the results of high trust selling can result in new levels of success in a matter of months, reaching a peak performance level isn't something that happens as a result of one good week of sales. High trust selling is a professional lifestyle that begins inside the heart of your salespeople and continues when they learn to find, acquire, and retain the best clients for your business. And that won't happen unless you empower them with the thinking, time, and tools to do so.

To this point in the book, you have been given the tools to create a rock-solid selling system for each salesperson on your team. Now your job is to follow up with them and follow through on what you've taught them to this point so that their sales success is not only imminent, but it's also permanent.

CHAPTER

FOURTEEN

The Law of the Encore

The Greater the Performance,
the Louder the Applause

Recently I took my wife, Sheryl, to see a concert of one of my all-time-favorite bands, Crosby, Stills, Nash, and Young. The show was incredible, and the encore, brought on by a prolonged standing ovation, was another show in itself. In fact, I was so excited about the performance that I drove 120 miles and took my brother to see the band perform again three nights later. The concert was just as good as the first one. And as if two concerts in four days wasn't enough—and it wasn't—three weeks later I flew two hours to a city three states away to see the final show of the tour with three friends.

As a result of how great the first performance was, I kept coming back for more . . . and more. And the same will be true of your clients if you are committed to following the Laws of high trust selling.

The fact is that behind every great performance is a passionate, motivated, and committed person—whether we're talking about a rock band or a real estate agent. Behind every bad performance is a bored, complacent, and indifferent person. And in the business of sales, you choose which you will be.

Becoming a highly trustworthy salesperson with a highly success-ful business is not anyone's responsibility but your own. You might have a bad boss, work for a poorly run company, have no leadership to guide you, sit in a five-by-five cubicle with paper flying over your head all day, or have only a phone and a table to your name. But you can rise above it all. It's been done before—by many of our students—

and it will be done again, every month, by salespeople who simply decide they are done with long hours, high stress, and mediocre sales success. It will be done again when *you* begin to take the steps necessary to elevate your sales efforts to the level of high trust. And while there, may be much that's required of you in the first few months to rebuild your sales business on a foundation of trust, I don't want you to get overwhelmed with the wealth of information contained in this book. Although it's essential for reaching your sales potential that you implement the principles and practices that we've discussed, I don't want you to finish this book without remembering, in the very least, two very simple truths: First, all sales happen as a result of trust—the higher the trust the greater the sales. And second, in the end, all high trust is a result of one thing: consistent, genuine service.

> **First, all sales happen as a result of trust—the higher the trust the greater the sales. Second, in the end, all high trust is a result of one thing: consistent, genuine service.**

WE'RE IN THE PEOPLE BUSINESS

As I've said before, high trust sales professionals have a different purpose than their counterparts. There is something bigger than the sale that motivates them to perform their best, and it's why every audience who takes in their performance is compelled to applaud. They are in the sales business for something more than the commissions they earn or accolades they receive. For high trust sales professionals it's all about people. In over 2,500 field calls and more than 350 interviews with high performing salespeople, I've noticed that the one thing that separates them from the lion's share of other salespeople is a burning desire to create an incredible service experience for every customer. The Law of the Encore says that the greater your performance, the louder your clients will applaud. And while your performance can be enhanced in many ways, the sum of a great performance is nothing more or less than great service.

CONTRASTS IN SERVICE

As you can imagine, I study service everywhere I go. I have seen the proverbial "good, bad, and downright ugly." I've seen sales professionals that genuinely care and genuinely add value. And I have seen salespeople who couldn't care less. And when you're on the other side of the transaction, the difference is quite evident.

Service Experience #1: Her name was Mona. It was a Sunday, and Sheryl and I were leaving for the Caribbean the following morning to host our Achieving Sales Mastery program at the Four Seasons Resort on the island of Nevis. But before we left I needed to pick up a couple of new pairs of pants. We buzzed over to Nordstrom after church and had arrangements to meet with Mona.

Upon our arrival, Mona introduced herself and immediately asked what our needs were. I told her, and the three of us went to that area of the Men's department. With Mona's guidance, we found a couple good pairs of pants, which I tried on. They fit great, except the hems were unfinished, as is usually the case for someone my height (I'm over six-feet tall). It was 11:30 A.M. and we were leaving the following day at 6:00 A.M. for Nevis, so out of concern I asked, "How soon could I get these hemmed?" She replied, "How soon would you like them?" I then confessed that we were leaving early the following morning and told her we would probably need them that same day. She made a quick phone call to the tailor and assured me that wouldn't be a problem. "They will be done by 5:00 P.M.," she confirmed, to my delight. Then without missing a beat she said, "Todd, you're probably going to be very busy packing for your trip, so rather than your coming back here, why don't I deliver them to your home by 5:00 P.M.? Would that be OK?"

"Wow, you will do that?" I replied, surprised.

"Absolutely," she assured me.

With Mona's assurance Sheryl and I were out the door without a worry. Mona had relieved us from any stress. She made doing business easy.

Later that day, Sheryl and I were in our bedroom packing our suitcases when the intercom at our gate chimed. I remember looking at my watch—it was 4:00 P.M. I pushed the intercom and heard, "Todd, it's Mona. I know that I am an hour early, but I have your pants." I buzzed her through the gate, and we all met at the front door.

"I'm pretty confident these will fit perfectly," Mona said as she handed me my pants, "but just in case, why don't you go try them on? The tailors are available until 9:00 P.M. if they don't fit."

At her suggestion I went back to the bedroom, tried them on, and sure enough, they were a perfect fit, as I knew they would be. I headed back to the entry, gave Mona the thumbs-up, and thanked her for her incredible service. I walked her outside and in our driveway I noticed an SL Mercedes convertible. I asked Mona, "Is that yours?"

"Yes," she answered.

"How can you afford a car like that?" I asked.

"By doing for all my clients what I just did for you."

"Why?" I asked.

"Todd," she said, "you are going to buy from me for the rest of your life. Sheryl is also going to buy from me. And that's very important to me. I want you to know that if we have it at Nordstrom, you can get it through me. And even if we don't have it, I will still get it for you." And then I understood why Mona is in the Pacesetter's Club, which means she sells over $580,000 in Nordstrom products per year.

As we walked around the back of her car, I noticed around the license plate a sign which read "SERVE." I also noticed that hanging in the back of her car were five more deliveries for other clients that day—Sunday. Then I knew she was right. My wife and I would never again buy from anyone at Nordstrom but Mona. We were her clients for life.

Service Experience #2: His name was Luís. Sheryl and I had just left the same resort in Nevis that we were traveling to five years earlier when we had met Mona. Our plane arrived in Puerto Rico, and we then boarded our flight to Dallas, our connection city for our final flight to San Diego. As we sat on the plane, I knew something was wrong; and I was correct. As the departure time came and went we all wondered what had happened. It was then that the captain got on the intercom and said, "Folks, there is nothing wrong with the plane, but in order to take off, we need a clearance from our maintenance center in the States and we will be ready to go. They are going to E-mail it down, then we will get it printed and be on our way." Sounded pretty simple. But almost ninety minutes later, when we were still on the ground, I began to wonder what the holdup was. Then we were told: There was only one printer, and it was broken.

We finally did get in the air, but at that point it was becoming clear to me that our connection in Dallas was going to be very tight. I figured out that if we landed on time, we should be able to get to the gate for our San Diego flight with twenty minutes to spare. Everything happened as planned, but just to be safe, we asked the attendant at our arrival gate to contact our departure gate to let them know we were on the ground and coming as fast as we could. The attendant made the call and we were off and running. Ten minutes later, we arrived at the gate, panting, and handed our tickets to Luís.

"I'm sorry," he said, "the flight is closed."

"What?" I shot back in shock. "The agent at the other gate called you and told you we were running to this gate!"

"I understand that," he said, "but the policy is that if you are not here twenty minutes before departure, your seats are in jeopardy of being given away."

"I have two full-fare first-class tickets," I replied, now frustrated. "I am also a VIP on this airline. You got a call from another employee informing you we were coming, and you gave my tickets away?"

"Sir," he said, "that's our policy, and this flight is full. As you can see, we are getting ready for departure and I can't put you on now."

"Can't you call the attendant and get my seats back?" I asked.

"No, sir."

"If the flight is leaving," I continued, "then why are they still loading baggage?"

"I don't know sir," he replied in monotone fashion. "That is a different department."

A half-hour later, forty minutes after we had originally arrived at the gate, the plane to San Diego was pushed back from the terminal without us on it.

Two hours later we boarded another plane to San Diego. The doors were latched and we were ready to be pushed back from the gate. But to my surprise, the door to the plane was opened and two passengers got on. The door was shut again. Five minutes later, it was opened again. The captain got on the intercom to let everyone know that the reason they opened the door twice was to accommodate passengers with tight connections. You can imagine my frustration.

A few days after arriving home, I sent a letter to the airline to let them know of my frustrating experience. A week later I received a form letter back with a credit to my mileage account of 10,000 miles. I don't know if you are familiar with mileage programs, but for someone who flies thousands of miles a year like I do, 10,000 miles is meaningless. It's the last thing I need. What Luís started, the customer service department finished; and as a result they lost a loyal customer. I have flown nearly 4 million miles on that airline; they were my carrier of choice. But because of one stupid move and an inability to come up with a meaningful solution, they have lost my business for life. And guess what else? They may also lose the people with whom I share that experience. In the end, poor service destroyed my trust in the airline. And they have done nothing to win it back.

THE COST OF BAD SERVICE

The contrasts in service that I shared with you are not exaggerated one bit. The bottom line is that through Mona, Nordstrom gained a client-for-life, and through Luís, that major airline lost a lifetime client. In the last chapter I showed you how valuable clients can be when you retain a high trust relationship with them for life. Hopefully, you are now convinced of your need to serve your clients continually in order to maximize client share. Now I want to show you what happens when you create dissatisfied clients so that you understand that high trust relationships are a treasure to be protected and cared for—even fought for when a mistake is made.

Using my company's products-value model from the previous chapter, let's start by assuming that the lost value of a loyal client is based on the fact that he or she will not buy from you again.

A. Satisfied Customer Value Lost	- $2,500
Indirect cost*	
B. Unhappy customer tells 10 people (A x 10)	- $25,000
C. 13% of "B" will tell as many as 20 people (1.3 x 20 x $2,500)	- $65,000
D. Total Indirect Cost	- $90,000
E. Revenue Lost From Negative Referrals (B + C x 50% assuming 50% don't buy that would have)	- $45,000
Total cost of one unhappy customer (A+E)	- $47,500

*Statistics are from the U.S. Technical Assistance Research Laboratories in Washington, D.C.

The bottom line is that it costs more to fall short of clients' expectations than to maintain relationships with them. In fact, it usually costs more to lose a client than it did to gain him in the first place. What I want you to understand is that once a high trust relationship has been built, it's not an option to just let it stagnate, or worse, do something to ruin it without trying to recover it. That could ruin your sales business and quite possibly your career. And the only way to avoid that happening is through a commitment to consistent value-adding service.

SERVICE IS THE UMBRELLA OF HIGH TRUST SELLING

If you remember from the first chapter, one of our students, Steven Marshall, reported an adjusted gross income on his 1992 tax returns of roughly $10,000—then jumped to an income of $800,000 just six years later. But that's not the whole story. Last year he doubled his income by earning $1.6 million in net commissions. And he did it by continually applying the same principles and practices you've learned in this book. He simply created high trust with one customer at a time, then implemented a system to consistently give every client brilliant, value-added service experiences. You see, serving your clients isn't another step in the high trust selling process, it's the embodiment of the high trust selling process—the culmination of a high trust performance deserving of an encore.

If you become a trustworthy salesperson, you can build a consummate sales business by adding significant value to your clients through world-class service.

All you've learned here boils down to this: If you become a trustworthy salesperson, you can build a consummate sales business by adding significant value to your clients through world-class service.

We've discussed how to be a trustworthy salesperson. We've talked about how to build a trustworthy sales business by giving top-notch sales performances and employing top-quality follow-up systems. The only thing left to discuss is how to keep your clients applauding on their feet even after you've conducted business. And that's a matter of service.

The following are eight ordinary steps to providing extraordinary service to your clients until the day you retire. Make these a part of your sales business creed and the umbrella to protect and sustain your new high trust enterprise.

Step #1: Decide how good you will be at client service. I'm serious. You must set your standards and know your expectations of yourself, because client service is a philosophy, not a department. Service is the heart of high trust selling, and it must be in your veins.

You are responsible for how your client is treated and no one else. Not another person or department in your company, not the post office, not Fed Ex, and not Xerox. You get the point. And the truth is that if you bought into the Law of the Shareholder, this will be an easy decision for you. As I have examined numerous high trust sales professionals, they have all settled on the heights of their client service standards. Needless to say, they're all shooting for the stars, and they all take full responsibility for the outcome.

I wasn't very bright early in my sales career, so I didn't understand this concept of client service. I remember one experience very clearly. I had failed to send paperwork for a sale to the right place at the right time, and my client was livid. She called on the phone and began cussing me out, telling me what a loser I was. She swore she would never do business with me again. I responded by telling her it wasn't my fault, that I wasn't the loser she thought I was, and that I didn't care if she ever gave me business again. We had this exchange, each time raising our voices, and in the end, she just hung up. I felt I had won. But I had actually lost. Within five days, four other clients that I was working with heard the story from her and my business dried up with all five.

Deciding how good you want to be at client service is truly your choice. No one will make it for you. Your company may tell you to be good at it. They may even train you to be good at it. But until you believe it on the inside, it will never manifest itself on the outside. Creating a great service culture and experience always starts with a vision. A vision is foresight, with insight, based on hindsight. Once you articulate your vision and put it in writing, your approach to selling will take on a whole new life and you will create a service culture that endears clients to you for good.

Step #2: Publish your core values and service standards. Make yourself accountable to your clients. Tell them what you are committed to doing up front. This is the Law of Leverage in action. You will be compelled to perform at the highest levels if your client-service values and standards are in writing, and shared with your clients. For example, here's a copy of what our client Tim Broadhurst shares with his clients.

Broadhurst & Co.
Core Values

The following principles represent the commitment we make to each client we are given an opportunity to serve. These principles have been established, affirmed, and are lived by each member of my very talented and very dedicated team.

We have decided that without exception we will

➢ ask questions and listen to our clients in order to fully understand their needs

➢ create mortgage solutions that complement our clients' overall financial strategy, and allow them to most effectively accomplish their short- and long-term financial goals

➢ be sensitive to the fears that many home buyers have about obtaining a mortgage loan and earn their confidence as a trusted advisor

➢ respect our clients' time and minimize the amount of effort required of them by applying our knowledge, experience, and resourcefulness

➢ use state-of-the-art technology to complement our customer service, making adjustments when necessary to avoid overwhelming our clients who are less technically proficient

➢ communicate regularly and proactively with our clients to keep them informed of the status of their loan and to reduce the stress that is associated with uncertainty

➢ ensure smooth, on-time closings with anticipated costs and terms

➢ provide our clients the luxury of home loans in the future with little effort on their part, by means of an Annual Mortgage Review

➢ measure our success by our clients' willingness to confidently recommend us

> take full responsibility for our actions and be honest at all times

> seek to improve the quality of service we provide by encouraging each client to critically evaluate our performance

> strive to honor God in all that we do

Once you have these values and standards published, guarantee the delivery of them. This is beyond your product guarantees. This is about your level of service. As much as possible, *take the risk out of doing business with you.* I have personally conducted over 3,500 seminars or private speaking events for small and large corporations. My company always has promised complete satisfaction, with specific elements of what we guarantee. Over the course of those events, I have spoken to over a million students. We have never been asked for a corporate refund and have not given more than ten public seminar refunds. When you offer a guarantee, it increases your commitment to deliver.

Step #3: Take only the business you can handle. If you can't serve clients the way they should be served, don't take their business. Make sure you know that you can deliver the service you promise before you generate a ton of business.

Recently we had one of the first reservations at a new, downtown San Diego restaurant. It was their first night of business, and my wife and I were excited to check it out. The owners had spent millions on their décor, tens of thousands on their advertising, and thousands on their employees. But things didn't exactly go over as they had planned with our service that night.

Sheryl and I were seated promptly, told of the specials, handed our menus, and asked if we'd like anything to drink. The drinks arrived and our waiter took our appetizer and entree orders. I ordered the rotisserie chicken and Sheryl ordered the mixed grill. So far, everything was going smoothly.

The appetizers came quickly, and our server said our entrees would be out in about twenty minutes. But twenty minutes came and twenty minutes went. At about the thirty-minute mark our server informed us that the cook was having a problem with the chicken and it wasn't done yet. He assured us it would just be another five minutes or so. No problem. We both ordered another drink and chatted as ten more minutes passed. By this time we were starting to wonder. About five minutes later, our entrees and drinks arrived—forty-five minutes past the time we ordered. Now, we've had to wait for good food before, so at this point we're not thinking the worst. But that would quickly change.

As I cut into my chicken, it exploded on my tie and suit. Did I mention that we were going to a play after dinner? Apparently, to accelerate the cooking process, the cook put the chicken in a steam pressure cooker and water got trapped between the skin and the breast meat. It wasn't a pretty sight. I glanced over at Sheryl and saw that she could barely cut through her steak. It was overdone. Apparently, it had waited patiently under the heat lamp as my chicken got motivated. I was not happy.

Fortunately for the restaurant, there's more to the story. And I will share that with you in Step 7. But where Step 3 is concerned, remember that you should never open your doors unless you are ready to deliver.

Step #4: Survey your customers before, during, and after the sale. If you publish your core values and service standards and share them with your clients, then you will always have a purpose for surveying your clients. One mistake sales professionals make—besides not surveying their clients at all—is only surveying after the transaction is complete and the sale is made. That's too late. If they are not happy at any point, and you go through with the transaction, you will have branded the negative experience on their minds. It's downhill from there.

Recently my wife and I bought a new Toyota Sequoia SUV from Toyota of Orange. Bar none, this was the most incredible service experience I've ever had. The dealership conducted an extensive interview on the front end that clearly created trust and led to our purchase. However, because we had special ordered, the delivery of the car was about two weeks away. Nonetheless, I was contacted multiple times between the order and the delivery. I received thank-you cards and calls before the car was even picked up. When I got to the dealership, Joe, the general manager, asked me about my experience to this point. I was told that Toyota would be doing a survey after the purchase and they wanted to know how I would respond if I were asked now. What could I tell them but that the experience had been seamless?

Bill, the sales professional, spent a half-hour with me showing me how to operate all the functions on the car and before I left asked if I had any additional questions. After I left he called me on my cell phone en route to ask how I was doing and if I had any questions. Three days later I received a thank-you card from the general manager, the sales manager, and my salesperson. Then I got a phone call from the dealership's customer service department. And a month after that, I received a survey from Toyota. After I turned the survey in, I received a beautiful document wallet for the glove compartment.

It doesn't matter if the sale is large, like a car, or small, like a nice dinner—the service experience can either make or break high trust. Sheryl and I were recently dining at a wonderful restaurant in San Diego by the name of Plateau. It had been an incredible experience to this point—smooth as silk. We were finished with our entrees and our server approached us with what looked like the bill. This was odd, I thought, until he said, "We really appreciate you coming in tonight. And we hope that you will come back. We know we have to earn your loyalty, so before I bring you your bill, I'd like to get you a complimentary dessert or after-dinner drink in exchange for your filling out this brief survey. Would you mind?" This was encore service at its best.

Step #5: Underpromise and overdeliver. One of the biggest mistakes salespeople make is overpromising and underdelivering. Don't tell clients their orders will be completed in a day if they might not be. Don't tell them you will be there at 6:00 P.M. if that's cutting it close. Never tell them you will call them back in five minutes. Never tell them it's $3,000 dollars and then charge them $3,200 dollars. High trust sales professionals don't need to do this. When you have an efficient system in place to determine and deliver solutions to your clients' needs, you will be able to accurately set and meet your clients' expectations without the need to offer unsubstantiated promises. And besides, if you've established high trust, you will not feel the need to overpromise in order to hold clients' interest. They trust you, remember.

Step #6: Know your impression points. This one's easy. Sit down for the next thirty minutes and make a list of the five to ten points in the sales process that the majority of your clients find most important. These will become the places in the selling process where you give your clients status updates to keep them very informed. For example, when the order has been submitted, let your client know. When the order is processed, let your client know. When the order is shipped, let your client know. Then automate this system and track these key points. What this does—particularly when you tell your clients up front that you will do this—is eliminate as much as possible your clients' anxiety and doubt.

Step #7: Master client recovery. One of the most overlooked service strategies for maintaining client loyalty is in the area of client recovery. Most salespeople don't know how to repair and recover relationships that have been damaged. But when you start seeing a service breakdown for one client as a 100 percent failure for that client, you will want to take steps to win that client's trust back.

Let me tell you a story about a client of ours named Tom Ward. For several years he and his team had been coming to our annual Sales Mastery Event. They easily invested $25,000 per year in our seminars and learning resources. But early on in my speaking career I let my ego get in the way of my purpose, and one particular year my head was a little too big from stage. Truth be told, I was a jerk. I didn't provide the same value for my students as I had in years past. I wasn't into my presentation. I sold product like a representative for Ginsu knives. Basically, I blew it and lost Tom and his team as a client. They were absent from our events for the next two years.

> ### *When you blow it with a customer, don't run from them. Run to them!*

Before I finish the Tom story, let me give you an example of how to recover a client by taking you back to the "chicken with an attitude."

Remember the chicken that exploded on my tie and shirt at that new restaurant? Here's what happened after that disastrous experience. The server apologized and told us to ask for him the next time so he could make sure that didn't happen again. Then he presented us with the bill. No discount. I was disappointed, so I sent a letter to the owner outlining what the food server should have done. They're the same actions you must take to recover a high trust client whom you've poorly served:

➤ Confess. Tell the client you blew it and apologize. No finger-pointing.

➤ Correct. Tell the client what you are going to do about it.

➤ Communicate. Let the client know you value him and that you want another chance, and give him an incentive to try you again.

The owner sent me a letter in which he:

➤ apologized and took full responsibility

➤ credited my Amex card for the amount of the meal and paid for dry cleaning my suit

➤ gave me a gift certificate for four without a monetary limit

And you know what? We went back, had incredible service, and have dined there many times since. It's one of our favorite restaurants. That goes to show that even when you do have a bad service day, an effectively recovered client can become one of your best.

Now, back to Tom, the man whose team I'd given a substandard seminar. I did the same thing with him that the owner of the restaurant did with me. I apologized, listened to what I should have done, dropped my ego, communicated my new commitment to him, and asked him to give us another chance. Today, Tom and I are best friends, and last year he was recognized for being my company's "Client of the Year," an award presented to the client who adds the most value to our company in terms of ideas that help us serve our clients better.

As much as it's within your power to carry out a task they request, always tell your high trust clients you can.

Step #8: Do whatever it takes. Don't tell customers you can't just because it's not "typical" or "normal." If you've done your homework, recruited and landed the best prospects, and secured high trust with a client, you have to remain committed to doing whatever it takes to keep them, like Mona at Nordstrom did for me. She didn't have to deliver the pants to my house. It was Sunday—the weekend. But she did because she recognized that it would add further value to me by letting Sheryl and me stay at home and pack for our trip. As much as it's within your power to carry out a task they request, always tell your high trust clients you can. Do whatever it takes to allow your clients to experience your unwavering commitment to provide for them exactly what they need and want, plus an additional 10 percent—every time. That's service excellence.

SELLING FOR LIFE

Now, you've come full circle. We've spent several hours together, discussing what it takes to become a person worthy of your prospects' and clients' high trust. We've talked about how to build a lasting, lucrative sales business on a foundation of high trust and under the umbrella of value-adding service. We've talked about a lot of steps and concepts that are vital to your success and satisfaction as a salesperson. But to this point, all we've done is talk. Now it's time to start walking down the high trust selling path.

There is nothing I can do to keep you from reading this book and still doing nothing different in your sales career. But I hope that's not the case, because the sales principles and practices that we've discussed will dramatically advance more than your sales career—high trust selling will dramatically improve your life. We're high trust salespeople now, and that means we don't sell just to sell. We're not in the sales profession just to get rich. We sell because we believe that what we do makes the lives of others better. We believe that when we partner with others—whether to provide copiers, cars, financial services, or homes—we offer them a more abundant way of working and living . . . and that gives us a more abundant career and life.

As high trust sales professionals, we know that true fulfillment comes as a result of having added significant value to others' lives, not just with the product or service we've provided, but also with the method in which we've communicated, the honesty with which we've conducted business, the integrity with which we've maintained the relationship, and the respect with which we've honored each individual. These are the things that make our profession one of the best there is. These are the things that make selling important. And these are the priorities that not only furnish us with more and more business; they give us more and more life.

In the end, selling only matters when it has given more life—to your clients and to you. I understand that now more than ever. As I finish writing this book, my wife Sheryl has just finished her sixth and final round of chemotherapy. Next week, she begins radiation treatment. A few months ago, when doctors discovered cancer in her body, it was one of the scariest moments of our lives. Since that day our lives and the lives of our four- and six-year-old sons have changed in ways we didn't think they would. But by the grace of God we were prepared. Not only as individuals who entrust our lives into God's hands, but also as a family who has at the top of its priority list, each other. Yes, I am a sales professional. But I'm not the same sales professional as I was twenty, ten, or even five years ago. Fortunately, there have been many points along the way where I've learned and applied the different lessons and principles we've discussed in this book. And nothing has been so important—especially in a time like this—than learning that there are things more important in life than what we sell. When selling complements those things, when selling adds value to the things that are most valuable in our lives and in the lives of our clients, then selling matters. Then selling is a true privilege. Then we can be both pleased and proud to be a sales professional.

Acknowledgments

A book like this doesn't happen overnight. In fact, this book has taken over thirty years to write. From the time I first sold candy door-to-door for Little League, my sales training had begun. I made a lot of mistakes as I learned the trade, and from the first sale until now I have become convinced that sales success does not happen accidentally. It happens by design. Many people had significant influence on me early in my career, and without them this book would not have been possible.

I can say without reservation that Norman Vincent Peale and W. Clement Stone contributed in a major way toward my success—and therefore this book—while I was still in my teens. Their works, *The Power of Positive Thinking* and *Success Through a Positive Mental Attitude,* rank at the top of my all-time must-read list for any salesperson striving for success.

Before I knew them as friends, Tom Hopkins, Zig Ziglar, Ken Blanchard, and Brian Tracy provided me with the ideas, knowledge, guidance, and coaching to succeed early on in my sales career. Their inspiration, sales and leadership training, and motivation gave me the constant lift I needed to soar high as a sales professional and business owner. Thanks to the four of you.

I would also like to thank my friend and colleague, Bill Bachrach, author of *Values Based Selling* and an early inspiration for many of the high trust principles that I have developed over the last fifteen years—your friendship is greatly appreciated.

ACKNOWLEDGMENTS

In 1996 I met a man by the name of Dr. John Maxwell. On January 14, 2000, we had dinner together and that evening changed the course of my future like no other evening. John has become a dear friend and mentor. As a result, I developed a relationship with Dennis Worden, who is now the president of The Duncan Group, and under his leadership the organization has achieved new heights of success. Dennis, thank you for your servant's heart and for your leadership commitment—you're making a major difference.

I want to say thanks to the entire Duncan Group team: to David, Chris, Matt, Peggy, Vivienne, Paul, Suzanne, Tiffani, Jonathan, Melony, Shelly, and my executive assistant, Amy, as they have unified under our common purpose and vision to utilize the principles of high trust selling to help tens of thousands of people each year take their businesses and their lives to new levels of success.

I would like to thank my writer, Brent Cole. You are truly a gift to our organization and me. To take my words and organize them into a comprehensive and compelling work is one incredible assignment. This book is a treasure chest of information because of what you did. I am blessed by our relationship, and I want you to know that on this and every other project on which we are partnering, you have taken us to a new level. For that I am very grateful.

Many thanks to my dear friend and business partner, Daniel Harkavy, President of Building Champions—your commitment to helping me finish strong is priceless.

Finally, to the tens of thousands of students who have proven that high trust selling works: I want to thank you for trusting me with your career and I encourage you to stay the course as you continue in your role of trusted advisor to your clients. May your journey be filled with more success and significance than you've ever dreamed.

About the
Author

inston Churchill once said this:

"Every day you may make progress. Every step may be fruitful. Yet there will stretch out before you an ever-lengthening, ever-ascending, ever-improving path. You know you will never get to the end of the journey. But this, so far from discouraging, only adds to the joy and glory of the climb."

➢ For the past 22 years, Todd Duncan has been engaged in the "joy and glory of the climb," helping mortgage professionals along their journey toward career and personal excellence.

➢ Todd's "ever-ascending" path has taken him from Rookie of the year, to top salesperson of the year, to today leading The Duncan Group, recognized as one of America's top sales training companies.

➢ He is the author of 5 books.

➢ Todd has conducted more than 3,500 seminars and workshops, impacting salespeople around the world; over one million sales professionals can attest to the effectiveness of Todd Duncan sales training, and many of these professionals have achieved documented gains of 28 percent to 300 percent.

➢ Todd stays current and "real world" by consistently interviewing top performers who earn between $250,000 and $2 million per year in commissions. And, in partnership with Building Champions, he consistently tracks sales training results, helping to build The Duncan Group into one of the most respected professional and personal sales training companies in America.

Live on the Edge!

Let Todd Duncan help you gain the selling edge! It's as simple as

1-2-3!

Step 1 After reading *High Trust Selling*, visit us online at **www.HighTrustSelling.com** and sign up for your FREE subscription to *Sales Wired*. This monthly, life-changing newsletter will keep you informed and focused on being your best!

Step 2 Download your FREE first audio lesson of *The Selling Edge*. Go to **www.HighTrustSelling.com** and begin your training now!

Step 3 Sign up for The Duncan Group's monthly sales training series, *The Selling Edge*. Todd's monthly CD and self-study guides will sharpen the reflexes needed to keep moving upward in the face of constant change and relentless competition.

Don't hesitate! Grab your edge NOW!
www. HighTrustSelling.com
Or call us toll free at 1-866-937-8633.

Do the events in your life occur randomly or by design?

Unfortunately most people live their lives simply reacting to events around them instead of proactively following a blueprint for success. After years of research, popular speaker and business leader Todd Duncan has found that by following five steps, we can build the life of our dreams.

In his gift book, *Life By Design*, Duncan encourages readers to undergo some necessary "remodeling" by:

Step 1 Pondering Your Plans (determining a plan for the life of your dreams).

Step 2 Finding the Right Lot (establishing the values/foundation upon which your life will be built).

Step 3 Drawing Your Dream Life (envisioning what your life will look like when it's built).

Step 4 Gathering Your Tools (determining the tools you'll need for construction).

Step 5 Commencing Construction (taking the initiative to begin the building process).

ISBN 0-8499-9588-4

COUNTRYMAN

Nashville

A Division of Thomas Nelson, Inc.
www.ThomasNelson.com

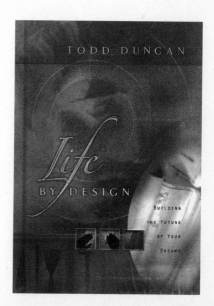